I WILL

By Ben Sweetland

You and Ben Sweetland are ready to start a wonderful journey — not just any journey, but your journey *of* success.

It is always your journey *of* success — never your journey *to* success. In Ben Sweetland's dynamic concept, success becomes a journey — never a destination. Success is all the blessings and good breaks that happen to you *on the way* — never what happens after you get there.

Whatever you want — more money — more energy — more friends ringing you up with happy invitations — more opportunity to advance in your work — all these, and more, are yours if you plan your journey *of* success wisely.

Ben Sweetland shows you how to plan your journey — step by step. Through his guidance you can make the exciting discovery of many joyous experiences in your life *right now*. You convert hopes into realities to change your whole life to fit the mold you want for yourself.

But the author doesn't stop at simply guiding you on your journey. He helps you take the next vital step — the step you need to jog you into action. He gives you practical, how-to-do-it-yourself suggestions.

His suggestions are in the form of specific affirmations. If you're after Better Health, A Business Of Your Own, Concentration — or any other goals — Ben Sweetland's affirmations will put your thinking on the right track.

Let Ben Sweetland's *I Will* show you the way to success *now — today*. It is your promise to yourself that you will find all those things you want most.

About The Author

Ben Sweetland is widely known on the West Coast as a consulting psychologist. One of his earlier books, *I Can*, has gone through eleven printings. He has also authored *Add Years to Your Life and Life to Your Years, Fourteen Golden Secrets, Magic Formula for Personal Accomplishment* and *Magic Formula for Selling.*

Books by Ben Sweetland

ADD YEARS TO YOUR LIFE; LIFE TO YOUR YEARS
I CAN!
14 GOLDEN SECRETS
MAGIC FORMULA FOR PERSONAL ACCOMPLISHMENT
MAGIC FORMULA FOR SELLING

I WILL

by **Ben Sweetland**

foreword by Melvin Powers

Melvin Powers
Wilshire Book Company

12015 Sherman Road, No. Hollywood, CA 91605

Wilshire Book Company edition
is published by special arrangement
with Prentice-Hall, Inc., Englewood Cliffs, N. J.

© *1960, by Prentice-Hall, Inc.*

Library of Congress Catalog Card Number 60-11162

Printed in the United States of America

ISBN 0-87980-083-6

Dedicated to Edel, who is my
little girl, my sweetheart
and wife.

FOREWORD

Not so many years ago, the repeated and often superficial declaration by an individual of the statement, "I Can," was hailed as a magical formula which would automatically start the wheels of success in motion.

No other more important factors, according to its optimistic proponents, had to underlie this dream-wish fantasy, and the constant repetition of the affirmation, no matter how loosely it was based on reality, was expected to bring the individual's chances for achieving his goals to full flower. The term was apparently supposed to act as both a synthesis and catalyst.

Alas, things did not turn out as expected for this unsupported euphoria. The slogan exempted the physiological effect of inertia and the psychological effect of procrastination. It was a visionary idea in that it failed to take into consideration the self-consistency theory of the late psychologist, Prescott Lecky, which argued that a careful evaluation of one's assets, both real and potential, had to precede a statement of intent.

I am reminded of the prevalence of this success formula by a friend of mine who remembers that the motto of his high school graduating class was "Success Comes in Cans." The principal suspected there was a frivolous notion behind the adoption of the motto, but he allowed himself to be persuaded it would provoke fruitful (if you will pardon the pun) discussion inasmuch as it coincided with the initial spurt to put everything edible that grew on trees into cans. A great variety of vegetables had already been canned, but T.V. dinners were still, thankfully, in the future.

My friend returned for the 25th anniversary of his class recently, and confided to me that a majority of it had evidently interpreted the motto more negatively or forgotten the promise of singular glory one feels in youth. Most of his former classmates indicated they were engaged in routine and unstimulating occupations, but the really amazing thing to him were the "reasons" they gave for the discrepancy between their jobs and the potential for high achievement implicit in their class motto.

It became apparent quite quickly that only a few of them were contented with their economic advancement or even pursuing the goals they had thought were attainable in their youth. Worse still, most of them had given up the idea that they ever would become an outstanding success. Many rationalizations were given to account for this lack of success, but rationalizations are never valid reasons. Reason implies logic, and there was no logic in their complaints.

Speculation seldom leads to provable answers except in scientific experiments where the same testing conditions can be maintained as long as necessary, but it is still possible, statistically, to determine what went wrong with the optimistic plans for the future of this average group of young graduates. Indeed, the fact that the group could be labeled as "average" offers the first proof that most of its members will always occupy routine positions.

Most of the group we are discussing had not gone on to college, but few high school graduates did in those days, yet their age group produced an unusual number of famous people. As a matter of record, a majority of high school graduates still do not go on to college although, admittedly, it is becoming increasingly difficult to obtain careers with an interesting and lucrative future without higher education.

Undoubtedly, Ben Sweetland, the author of this book and a highly successful career consultant, would speculate that most of those in my friend's class had been unsuccessful because they had not recognized the vastly different results that occur when "I Will" is justifiably substituted for "I Can." There is a great deal more than a semantic difference.

It is relatively easy for an individual, even an honest one, to say he can do something even though he has never put himself to the test. We all fight feelings of inferiority, and it is natural to say a certain objective is within our power to accomplish, particularly if we do not have to prove our ability by initiating proper action *at once.*

We are even more optimistic about our talents if proof of them can be postponed into the dim and remote future. After all, we tell ourselves, things *could* turn out the way we want them to, and in the meantime we can do something easier while we wait for the happy but unlikely set of circumstances that will allow us to achieve our most cherished goal.

This is a face-saving philosophy, of course, because it allows us to blame fate for our failures, but the fact is fate seldom has anything to do with our success or failure. People, to a large extent, create their own fate.

Contrast now, if you will, the individual who says he *can* do something with the confident and prepared individual who tells himself he *will* do anything that is required of him to reach his goal. The former is indicating a certain, or even uncertain, potentiality while the latter is stating he is going to take action immediately about this possible potentiality so that it will become more tangible than a premonition. It is a "put up or shut up" situation.

"Getting started on anything is difficult," Mr. Sweetland admits, "but it will be easier if you look on success as a journey, not a destination." There is a valuable truth in this statement, and it will grow more valuable as you think of its many meanings.

It was Mr. Sweetland's opinion that most people do not become a success because they think of it as a destination, perhaps years removed from the present, and to be attained by surmounting innumerable obstacles. The point of his book is that achieving success does not have to be *that* difficult.

Most of you already know that it is pleasant and invigorating to conquer a difficult problem. What apparently many individuals do not know is that greatness is measured by one's willingness to grapple with a number of such problems—*one at a time.* Heed those italicized words because many people think they can do more than one thing at a time. It is true you can try, but you will usually wind up doing justice to none. The invigoration one feels from solving one's problem is strong enough to help in conquering the next, and so it goes, hopefully, to no foreseeable end.

We have an adage, "Nothing succeeds like success," to explain this phenomenon, but most people never think they have reached the point where this truism will work for them. The real problem, of course, lies in making a start or, as Mr. Sweetland would say, "beginning your journey."

It should be perfectly clear that success cannot succeed itself unless there is some success to start with. You must provide the initial success, but it need not be on a large scale to activate the success formula which then provides most of its own impetus.

"This nation," the late Dr. Norbert Wiener once said, "is becoming more and more a victim of the 'numbers' game." A larger number of dollars, men and facilities are expected to solve everything. Actually, this game is played not so much to win as much as to provide great noise and fury, and shield, by the large number of players, those who are playing a different game entirely.

Too many people today, confused by the entropic commotion all around them, tell of the big things they would like to do rather than do the little things that must provide the knowledge and confidence which underlie achieving the escalated goals they seek. They do not, of course, really seek these goals or they would be doing something more active toward attaining them than indulging in wishful thinking.

The Great American Dream, whatever that term may mean to each individual, is still attainable, but it must come from individual effort. It is not something you are entitled to, regardless of what the politicians say, and you must work for your particular version of it to come true. In addition, your efforts must be within a social framework that helps others to realize their dreams.

I was especially impressed, in reading this book, by Mr.

Sweetland's use of the term, "Happy Discontent." Those who are the most successful are never thoroughly contented. If they were, there would be no need for them to do anything more—today, tomorrow, next week or ever.

The progress of our nation thus far has pointed up the fact that "Necessity is the mother of invention." Philosophically, the completely contented individual would never feel the pangs of necessity, and would never make further progress in any direction.

One of the real dangers to any nation is that its more aggressive members will fashion an environment which offers no apparent challenge to the individual. I use the word "apparent" because the challenge is still there, buried beneath material benefits which stultify ambition and make change difficult.

There are today millions of people who complain that they have no future, that everything has already been done. They say this despite the fact that we are beset on all sides by problems they could help solve by remembering that no machine or government is better than its weakest link.

Arnold Toynbee, the famous British historian, writes that human beings cannot flourish if their natural environment is too easy or too rigorous. The answer is the same although the environments are totally different. There is no all-consuming desire to go forward by changing the environment, whether it be too bountiful or too forbidding. Inertia operates in each case.

The point I am trying to make is that the average individual loses a great deal of his ambition to change the world as soon as he has enough of the world's goods himself. His real potential is smothered under the trivia we have blindly come to consider are manifestations of success. Another rich man has been born who will struggle no longer to right wrongs by espousing causes. He becomes complacent, the worst of all deterrents to creative action. Unlike "yon Cassius," he loses that "lean and hungry look" which always has been the precursor of "a better mouse trap."

In this age of alienation and depersonalization, the question of whether you can do something is beside the point. The real question is whether you will. From the I-Thou philosophy of Martin Buber to Dr. Leslie H. Farber's I-It essays on the will[1], published recently by Basic Books, thoughtful men today are concerned with man's will.

Dr. Farber puts the will under a miscroscope when he states that our collective anxiety is due to attempting to will what cannot be willed, even in the face of a threat to our existence. This is a complicated statement, but surely there is one threat to our existence we all recognize, and we can no longer will to what use it will be put. The optimist can hope and the religious man can pray, but an act of sheer will can no longer protect us from the atomic bomb or other proliferations of subsidized science whose secrets are invariably fathomed by other scientists because pure science is impersonal.

But man can help himself, no matter what the situation. Whether you are interested in saving yourself, the world or both, your will is the deciding factor in most of the situations you will encounter.

There are still many things we must learn about the will, but Mr. Sweetland tells you how you can be rewarded by its most simple usage. It is never too late (or too early) to start saying you will accomplish certain ends if that possibility actually exists.

Good luck on your journey, but try never to reach an ultimate destination. If you do, your importance to the communion of man is ended.

Melvin Powers
Publisher

12015 Sherman Road
No. Hollywood, California 91605

[1] *The Ways of The Will: Essays Toward a Psychology and Psychopathology of Will*, Dr. Leslie H. Farber, Basic Books, 1966

CONTENTS

SUCCESS IS A JOURNEY

You are about to begin what can be the most important journey of your life. A venturing of the mind and the spirit, it will teach many priceless things full of wonder, of simplicity, value, and wisdom. There will be no real trains, ships or planes to be sure, yet this excursion discovering life's riches will be more vivid and real than any journey you have ever taken—and one you will never forget.

A questionnaire sent to 1,134 men and women asked the simple question: "Is success a destination or a journey?"; 926 said it was a *destination*.

There in a single dramatic example is the reason why so few men and women have the courage to attempt the climb to success. Viewing success as a destination gives one the feeling that to reach it, he must ascend over tortuous paths and that the journey will be a long and trying one. This, of course, is not true. Success is *not* a destination. It is a journey.

If you are taking a trip—to Hawaii, let us say—does your enjoyment come only after you have arrived in the islands? Not by any means.

Your joy comes the moment you decide to take the trip. As you go to a travel agency to get descriptive folders, you are happy in anticipation of the journey. Packing your bags gives you a thrill because, as you carefully insert each garment, you visualize yourself wearing it, either on shipboard or after arrival, on some festive occasion.

On the day of sailing, you reach the ship early and with a group of well-wishing friends go to your cabin where you joyfully inspect your *bon voyage* remembrances.

The ship sails, and each day is replete with a wide variety of fun-packed activities, which keep up until the guy ropes are tossed ashore at Waikiki.

And, does your enjoyment end as you reach your destination? Not a bit! It's not only the things you do in Hawaii which give you happiness—but the return will be packed with pleasure.

Upon arrival the chapter is not closed by any means. The memories, the conversations regarding your cruise, your increased knowledge of other places beside your own, all tend toward returning tangible dividends of satisfaction as a result of the trip.

Attaining success is not a destination—it is a journey. You start your journey the moment you determine to be a success. This means that it is not necessary to reach the pinnacle of success before you begin enjoying it. You gain happiness after taking the first step toward success.

Here is a little understood fact. You *are* a success the moment you start on the road to success. Therefore, you do not have to wait until you have money in the bank, nor your bills all paid before you are a success. You can be a success *right now*.

To Create Is to Live

I have written many articles on hobbies—and mostly from a psychological standpoint. I pointed out that creation is the foundation of our existence—that we are *creatures* (the products of creation); and that unless we are continually creating, we are not conforming to the laws of nature.

Success, in itself, is not soul satisfying. To arrive at the summit with a pot of gold might give temporary pleasure but, in no time at all, one would reach a state of boredom.

Achieving through creating is the epitome of satisfaction. Therefore, to start on the road to success through creative efforts means that from the moment you set your plans in motion, your enjoyment begins.

Do you now comprehend the significance of the statement: "Success is a Journey"? Do you understand that this journey can begin any time you say, meaningly, I WILL make the start?

And need the day of starting be some time in the undetermined future?

Reading this book can be considered as being preliminary to your departure into the realms of accomplishment, power, leadership—Happiness.

An Unusual Request?

I want *you* to feel that reading *I WILL* is the greatest step you have ever taken in your life and, perhaps, the most important step you will ever take.

This can be true and it *will* be true if—and here is a most vital word "IF"—if you accept the book in the spirit that it WILL be the most important step of your life.

In just a moment, I am going to make a most unusual request.

A good percentage of people read formulas for self-improvement, and while doing so will think of many Tom, Dick and Harry's who should read them—but they seldom apply the thoughts to themselves.

I want *you* to imagine that this book was written, specifically for you. Every chapter, every paragraph, every sentence and every word was intended for you. Forget about the other fellow. This is a session which you personally, are having with the author and every line your eyes follow will be fitted into your own life.

Now, here's the unusual request! *Unless you seriously intend applying the principles which will be given to you—please do not read any further.* Give the book to a friend, or, if you have purchased it with a return privilege, ask for your money back.

Thousands of letters from readers of other books of mine clearly indicate that the books have been of great value. Many letters tell of revolutionary things happening in the lives of the writers. But I also have information to the effect that some have read the books without concentration in the same spirit they read novels. They might enjoy them, feeling they contain good sound common sense but they usually fail to grasp the motivating force of the messages given.

There are no principles in these pages which have not been

proved and which cannot and will not be proved again. There is no conflict with any type of religious belief. Every suggestion given will be accompanied with a reason *why* you should accept it, and the results you have a right to expect from so doing.

I Can Versus I Will

It has been said that the basic difference between the success and the failure is that one man thinks in terms of I Can't—and the other of I Can. This is partially true and, as I say this, I am not unmindful of the fact that I have used the expression countless times in my writings, my lectures and my radio and television programs.

To be successful, you must *know* that you *can* be successful. This is important—mighty important. In fact, it is absolutely necessary. But, knowing you *can* do a thing is no indication that you *will* do it.

I maintain that you *can* do anything you make up your mind you want to do. You *can* climb high in your job. You *can* build a successful business of your own. You *can* become a great writer. You *can* become a famous painter. You *can* become an outstanding singer, or musician. You *can* climb to high levels as a lawyer, doctor or architect. But *will* you? This is the determining question.

Using an understandable illustration, I might say that building an "I CAN" consciousness is the motivating force which loads the gun; an "I WILL" determination is the detonator which fires the gun. Both forces are necessary. The gun would be worthless without either of them.

An acquaintance once called upon me to unload a tale of woe. He contemplated suicide.

"My family would be better off without me," he wailed. "Were it not for the money my wife earns, we would starve. Should I die, they would have a little insurance money and would not have the responsibility of supporting me," he added mournfully.

I sat this man down at an unused desk, gave him a pad and pencil, then suggested:

"John, suppose that some millionaire would make you this

unusual proposition: He would tell you that if at the end of a year you had paid all of your bills and had a good income, he would give you a million dollars,—what would you do?"

I told John to take his time and see what he would work out. Believe it or not, at the end of an hour this man had developed a most logical plan for re-establishing himself.

"Why don't you do it?" I asked with elaborate casualness. John did. The last I heard of him, he had a good income and was not only out of debt, but had bought a most livable home for himself and his family.

Here is a case where a man had an "I CAN" consciousness— he proved that he knew what could be done—but he had not built up an "I WILL" determination.

I might relate another interesting story.

Mary J. had a mind filled with ideas—good ideas. During a visit, she told of case after case where her ideas had been successfully used by others. She had made nothing through these ideas. It was just that she had procrastinated in doing anything about them herself and later others had conceived the same things.

I asked Mary why she had not acted upon her ideas at the time they were conceived. She gave me one reason after another —none of which was valid.

To prove of help to Mary, I took one specific idea of hers and used it as a subject for analysis.

I asked this creative woman to name the reasons why she did not make use of the idea.

"I lacked sufficient money to develop it," she answered.

"All right," I ventured, "how would you go about solving that problem?"

She reflected a moment, then came up with a most plausible solution. Mary could adjust her living budget so that she could lay aside about 10 per cent of her income. Also, she knew ways and means of making a tidy bit of money during her spare time.

I asked questions as to the steps she would take in developing the idea; where she would take it after it had been developed, and many others. In every case, after thinking about the question for a few moments she would come up with logical answers.

Now then, why had this lady permitted one idea after another to drift from her and eventually be used by others?

She had the "I CAN" spirit, but *not* the "I WILL" determination.

You might wonder how you would find all the answers regarding an objective, even if you did build up an I WILL determination. And this would be a good question.

Once you have an objective and *know* you CAN accomplish it—then determine you WILL and things begin to happen. First you study the obstacles standing between you and the attainment of your objective, and then you work out a plan of action which will enable you to hurdle those obstacles and attain your objective. We will go into this subject more specifically in a later chapter.

Why Do People Fail?

When giving formulas for success, the one who is a failure will invariably make all sorts of statements to justify his lack of success.

In view of what I have given so far, a natural question from a mind which is inclined to be a bit skeptical would be: "Those who have started out to accomplish something and then failed have disproved your theory. Didn't they first have an 'I WILL' determination before they started and, if so, why did they fail?"

Let's suppose you were going on a long motor trip. In order to assure its success, you would prepare yourself for every phase of the trip. You'd check your car thoroughly to make certain it was in first class condition: good tires, brakes, etc. You would want to know that your motor was properly tuned. You would determine to drive carefully so that there'd be no accidents. The clothing to wear, the amount of money to carry, all of these things would be carefully considered. At the end of the journey, you could look back over a happy, successful trip. You see? You not only had the "I WILL" attitude regarding going on the trip, but you took all of the steps necessary to assure it being a successful trip.

There is a reason for every failure. It isn't because the wheel of fortune passed by a person's number, meaning that he wasn't destined to be a success. It is because, in some respect, he did not do the things essential for success.

The Anatomy of Success

So far, we have learned that the vital elements of success are:

1. Know that I CAN be a success.
2. Determine I WILL be a success.
3. Develop a plan of action based upon an understanding of the obstacles standing between you and your objective.

The rest of this volume will be devoted to a revelation of ways and means of (1) developing an I WILL attitude and, (2) learning what you must know—and the things you must do to successfully back up your I WILL determination.

Are You Contented with Your Life as Is?

If your answer to this question is yes, you need read no further. I doubt, however, that this is true. If it were, there would be little reason for you to even consider reading this book.

If you are not a financial success; if you have not done the things you would like to do; if you have not reached a position of importance and respect; if every new day does not open with thrilling anticipation . . . then the very book you are holding in your hands will be as a magic wand—poised to usher you into a land of dreams come true.

Be happy even if your life has been disappointing. Rejoice if life's greatest objectives are still ahead of you. Give thanks for the past dreams which failed to come true. Why all this cheering for past failures? This cheering is because of the new and exciting experiences yet to come.

My greatest success has been in my later years of life. Had my blessings come to me 30 or 40 years ago, they would be commonplace now. Now, each day, as something new comes into being, it is enjoyed to the fullest. In fact, I am kept young in anticipation of all of the wonderful things which are coming to me.

Success a Journey

In the beginning, you were told that success is not a destination, but a journey. This being true, you do not have to wait for the accumulation of wealth before gaining happiness, because your thrills begin the moment you start your journey.

You are soon to make the start. In some respects the journey will be an imaginary one, yet, in all your life, you have never been on a trip which has given you even a small fraction of the happiness and satisfaction you will get from this one.

As I think about it, the journey you are about to take is *not* an imaginary one. It will be as real as life itself. Webster defines journey as going from one place to another. This is exactly what you are about to do. You will be journeying from the common*place* up and onward to the realm of joyous, carefree, abundance.

Up to this point, I have been referring to the work you are reading as a *book*. It is more than that. Think of it as a medium through which you are receiving the esoteric wisdom which will distinguish you from the average individual.

Does this last statement sound egotistical? It is not meant to be. During the last several years of my life, I have risen from mediocrity to a place where I am enjoying luxuries I did not even dare to dream about in my younger days. My estate was not inherited. Every iota of it was acquired through the use of the principles now being given to you.

As I write this, frequently gazing through the picture windows in my study looking out over our wide expanse of lawn toward the majestic oak trees which form a canopy over our driveway, I feel grateful and inspired. I feel as though a divine power is guiding my hands in expressing the thoughts which *you* can use to bring you the type of happiness with which I am so abundantly blessed.

Perhaps one of the reasons why I am inspired is because of my love of people. Although I have probably never seen you and may never see you, I want to give you a new zest for life, a firm realization that life is what you make it and a determination that you WILL make it beautiful.

It is your rightful heritage that you not only possess the necessities of life, but a generous share of the luxuries. It is intended that you have Peace of Mind, which is the Alpha and Omega of all objectives.

Yes, my friend, you are going on a journey. It will be a glorious journey, because you will make it so.

As this chapter comes to a close, may I make a suggestion? Before turning the page, will you read this chapter again? Here's why. You started reading with a mind of curiosity; interested, primarily, in learning what it is all about. By now you sense that in and between the lines is a dynamic force which can make all of your days from now on exciting and happy.

After you re-read this chapter, relax and close your eyes for a few moments. Realize that you are about to start a journey. Visualize yourself moving into a new life where you are master of circumstances and not a slave to them. See yourself acquiring those things which will make you happy and which will enable you to make those near and dear to you happy.

See yourself gaining the respect and admiration of those with whom you come in contact.

•   •   •   •   •

Are you ready for the next chapter? Would it be better to wait a day before reading it so that you can meditate and contemplate over what you have read? You be the judge, my friend. Remember, however, from this moment on, you and I are genuine friends. I am going with you on this journey. Hand in hand, and with hearts overflowing with joy, as our vehicle proceeds we will witness new vistas of grandeur opening up before us.

•   •   •   •   •

Yes, *you* are going on a journey.

MAPPING YOUR JOURNEY

For the next ten minutes, I want you to live in the land of make-believe.

When you were a child, do you remember the games of "Make Believe" you would play? For example, you'd "Play House" and imagine yourself as being an adult and do as an adult would do. For the time being, you *would* be an adult, at least so far as your imagination was concerned. You would *see* yourself fully grown and doing the things you might do, were you full grown. There were no limitations. You could experience anything within the limits of your powers of imagination. You could own and drive a fine car. You could have imaginary servants—and give them commands.

Right now—you are to unshackle your imagination and give it full reign.

Think of yourself as starting to plan a journey—a trip to the land of "Dreams Come True." Think of yourself as having been singled out by Fate as the recipient of an endowment in which you have fallen heir to everything you feel stands between you and your complete happiness and peace of mind.

If you are a man, you might have envied those men who, through their success, are able to provide their wives and families with the comforts and luxuries of life. They live in fine homes with servants. They drive the latest and best automobiles. Their loved ones dress well. There is always plenty of money for travel and to put the children through fine schools and universities.

If you are a woman, you may have cherished your dreams of being a career woman—perhaps as a noted writer or a great designer. Or, your thoughts may have strayed toward the stage, screen or TV, giving you visions of yourself as an outstanding actress. Again, it could be that your ambition is to develop a personality, so radiantly magnetic that you will attract the type of a man who could and would provide you with the better things in life.

Yes,—for the moment you are to live in the land of Make Believe. You are about to depart from the world which you have accepted as one of drudgery, failures and disappointments, and arrive in your own envisioned Utopia.

Planning Your Journey

All successful journeys are planned. If we contemplate an ocean voyage, it is customary to visit a travel agency and select one or more printed folders describing the country, or countries, we intend to visit. We may also secure folders describing the liner and the accommodations we wish to reserve. We consider the wardrobe we'll take, the luggage we'll need, etc.

If our trip is to be by train, we get time tables so that we may compute our departure time and select the train on which we'll return.

Should we use an automobile for our transportation, most likely we will visit our auto club for the purpose of obtaining maps and road information.

In other words, if we are experienced travelers, we anticipate every condition we may encounter, and be prepared for it.

You are about to begin the most exciting journey of your life—a trip you'll never forget. The day you are reading this will be recorded in your memory as the day you really began to live. You'll be glad for all your experiences of the past because they will offer so much contrast with those to come.

So, according to what you have learned so far, what is the first thing you should do? *Plan your journey,* of course.

To encourage you—and to let you know you *can* change your life through a change in mental attitude, permit me to tell you a true story:

For many years I conducted classes on applied and creative psychology in a well known college. The principles on which I spoke were no different than those you are about to read.

A young man (John Green, I'll call him) subscribed for a

series of lectures. John was working for a small salary, had no money saved up, and did not dare to think of marriage because he was not doing a very good job taking care of himself. He wondered and worried about how he could add the expense of a wife and home.

It was not too difficult to convince John that he had everything necessary to make him a success—and that it did lie within the realm of possibility for him to become a success, but he had not reached the point of enlightenment where he could actually *see himself* as a success.

But, John went on the journey *you're* about to take. At this point I'll not tell you the things he did because I would be repeating the instructions which are just ahead of you. But I will tell you a bit about the John Green of today.

After John found himself living in a world of abundance, one where he could select whatever his heart desired, he began building the kind of life often dreamed of, but seldom realized.

He found the girl who, for him, was ideal, but he did not want to ask her to marry him until he could take her into a fine home which would be their own. An architect was employed, exciting plans were drawn and it wasn't too long until John carried his bride over the threshold of a most delightful home— elegantly furnished. In addition to maintaining a high standard of living, John has built up a worthwhile bank account. He has taken his wife on several trips including Bermuda and Europe— and, I learned, made his wife a Christmas present of nothing else but a glorious mink coat.

John Green's experience can be duplicated by you. There is only one determining factor as to the height to which you may climb—and that is the scope of your imagination. In formula form, I might say: *See yourself as you want to be: know you can reach the level to which you aspire—and, through the I WILL spirit built upon the premise yet to be described, take the simple steps necessary to bring your plans into fruition.*

All right! Let's plan your trip. But first, where do you want to go? The answer to this question will encompass a list of objectives covering your desires for material acquisitions, improvements you would like to make in your physical being and changes you would like in your affairs.

In laying out your journey, you go about it in a painstaking, methodical way. This is the most important journey of your life, and you will want to have it carefully—yes, scientifically, planned.

If you wanted to remodel a building, you would, undoubtedly, call in an architect to lay out the plans for you. And, what are the steps the *architect* takes? The first thing he would do would be to determine what he would like to accomplish. He would think of the things which should be removed from the building so that he could carry out his plans for remodeling. In other words, he would have to begin tearing down before he could build up.

This is the plan you will follow in reconstructing your life. You will decide on what you *do not want* before determining what you *do* want.

I believe in visualization. I like to put my plans on paper so that I can study and perfect them. And, referring back to the architect, can you imagine him designing a building without putting his plans on paper? Even a remodeling job is carefully worked out on the drafting board.

So, let's list the objective we intend to bring into being. Since we are thinking in terms of a tour, we might think of each objective as a station on our journey. Following is a typical objective chart, divided into the three divisions already named. This one might not apply to you at all—your objectives might be entirely different. But, before proceeding further, take a sheet of paper and rule it into three columns and make your objective list. It will act as a starting point for your journey.

OBJECTIVES

Material Possessions	*Physical Being*	*Affairs*
New home	Better health	Respect of all
Fine furnishings	Less or more weight	Leadership
Fine new automobile	Better memory	Prestige job
Big wardrobe	Concentration	Respect of family
Financial security	Ability to relax	
	Master of habit	
	Happiness	
	Peace of mind	

You Receive a Legacy

Suppose you would hear from a lawyer and his letter would tell you of a big legacy which was coming to you. In the letter is a list of the various properties to which you have fallen heir. How would you react? Would you casually read the letter, then lay it aside as you do with most letters? You know better. You would read it and re-read it, and re-read it again—each time finding your spirits rising still higher. This is exactly how I want you to react regarding your list of objectives—*because they can and will come into being,* if they are at all within reason.

All right—now we will get back to your journey. Your trip has been decided upon. The land you'll reach will prove to have new horizons of accomplishment and attainment. There you will find awaiting you the various objectives you have selected—and more. Because due to your growth through the development of your ability to acquire whatever you desire, you will raise your sights to new levels of achievement.

You learned in the beginning that success is not a destination. It is a journey.

With your list of objectives, it would be no fun at all if you should attain them all at once. Yes, it would be interesting at the time, but you would soon be taking all of them for granted and they would not mean much to you.

If you think of success as a journey and keep arriving at your objectives one at a time, you would live through a succession of thrills. Life, as you reach objective after objective, would grow into an ecstatic series of anticipated events.

Check Your Emotions

Up to this point, what is your emotional reaction? Do you have the feeling that you are reading an interesting book—one you'll read through to the end? If this is true, read no further than this chapter. You are not getting from it that which has been intended for you.

On Christmas morning, have you ever had the opportunity of watching a child as he sees his array of gifts for the first time? As he opens package after package, there is an indescribable glint in his eyes. You can actually sense the joyous emotional glow radiating from every fibre of his being.

If I am succeeding in putting my message across to you—this is exactly how you should feel right now.

You should actually become unaware that you are reading but, as your eyes eagerly follow the lines, instead of words, your mind's eye sees yourself—like the butterfly emerging from its chrysalis—entering into a new realm of exultant living.

Perhaps up to now you have been wishing for a better life. This is all over with now. No more wishing. If you have developed the right spirit, you *know* what is ahead of you. Like Archimedes, upon discovering a method of determining the purity of gold, you want to throw open your arms and shout to the world "Eureka!"

The title of this book: I WILL! is more than a name designating its contents. It is a declaration of intention. It is your pledge to yourself that *you will* carry through in accepting and following the suggestions given and yet to be given.

"I've read dozens of the best inspirational and self-help books, —yet I fail to get results," a recent visitor insisted emphatically.

I asked him what he wanted to accomplish. He wasn't quite sure. All he could be specific about was his dissatisfaction with his life as it existed.

Here was a man who wanted to improve himself—yet had no plans as to the changes he would like to make.

If you want to plant a garden—you do not take a handful of seeds of all kinds and throw them into the ground. No—you first decide on what kind of flowers you would like to have. You obtain the proper seeds or plants. Then you follow the instructions as to the things you should do to raise successfully the flowers you have selected.

Referring once more to the architect—he would not attempt construction of a building without detailed plans as to how it should be built. He determines in advance every item which will enter into the construction of the building.

Perhaps for the first time you will design your future life according to plan. The purpose of this book is to help you in this planning and to lead you confidently toward a well balanced life. There is no disputing the fact that in our society this means money is necessary. To enable you to maintain a high standard of living you will require plenty of it—and you can get it. But never forget that wealth, by itself, is no assurance of happiness. Some of the most miserable people I know are rich in worldly goods and bankrupt in life's non-negotiable riches.

You want the admiration and respect of all those with whom you will come in contact. You will build a personality so magnetic, people will be attracted to you and will want to do things for you.

You will want radiant mental and physical health. You'll want to awake in the mornings with that glad-to-be-alive feeling. Your attitude toward your physical being will be such that you could take years off of your looks and add them to your life. You may grow more youthful, and your face may become more beautiful as it reflects the beauty of your thoughts.

Make Haste Slowly

By now, your anxiety to delve into the chapters ahead should be almost irresistible. You can hardly wait to start on the journey you have been mapping for yourself—but take it easy. I have an important suggestion to make before you read a line in the next chapter.

Do me the favor of holding back about two days before you approach Chapter 3.

Here is what I want you to do. Begin a program of visualization. Review your objectives—then start seeing yourself as having them. Is it a new home you want? Visit the type of a neighborhood in which you would like to live. Go through some of the model homes—or homes which are for sale. Picture in your mind the exact home you enjoy owning—and hold the thought that such a home will be yours. *Do not wish for such a home!* Know you are entitled to it and that it *will* be yours.

Would you enjoy driving one of the new high-powered automobiles? Visit automobile row and inspect the various cars. Find the one which would make you happy—then *know* that it will not be long before such a car will be adorning your garage.

Visit the furniture stores, the clothing shops, the jewelers.

See the things you have always wanted—and know that now they can, and *will*, be yours.

Do not try to figure out reasons why you can not possess the objectives you have set for yourself. The failure is always finding excuses as to why he failed; never giving any thought to steps he could take to become a success. The success, on the other hand, if he finds one method will not work—instead of stopping and admitting failure—will find another course to pursue so that he will succeed.

A woman living in Chicago had always bemoaned the fact she could not move to California where she would like to live.

"Why don't you move to California?" I asked her. She looked at me as though I was talking in riddles. Then she went into a long dissertation as to why such a move was impossible.

I asked this woman to be specific as to why she could not move to California. She gave many reasons, the most important being she did not have the money. Also, she explained, she knew no one in California and was afraid she would not be able to find a job if she made the move.

I asked her to name a few ways whereby she could add to her income and accumulate enough money on which to make the change. After a moment's reflection, she came up with some practical ideas. I asked her how she would go about making friends in California—and the steps she would take in getting a job. In due time she answered these questions in a very satisfactory way.

I have resided in California for many years in the suburbs of San Francisco. One day I received a telephone call from this same woman, enthusiastically telling me that she had moved to California and had already landed a good job.

What had been holding this woman back? She had not developed an I WILL attitude. She proved that she knew what she should do—but had not gotten herself in an I WILL frame of mind.

You have been mapping the journey you are about to begin —a journey into a land of adventure, accomplishment and above all happiness.

You will make this a successful journey because you are taking exceptional care in planning your journey.

PREPARING TO START
YOUR JOURNEY

It's time to pack your bags! And what you take with you will have a definite bearing on how much you will enjoy your journey.

A young couple once told me of their first, long anticipated vacation and how it was marred because of their haste in packing. Driving through the mountains, they saw a big mother bear with her baby bear. "What a picture that will make!" excitedly exclaimed the husband. The wife, embarrassed, admitted she had forgotten to include the camera.

From the summit a most delightful view of the valleys below could be had. They wanted to get the most out of it—but found they did not pack their binoculars.

They did not have their heavy shoes for mountain hiking. In fact, their many oversights were constantly casting shadows on what had been anticipated as a wonderful vacation.

This will *not* happen to you. You are about to start on the most important—and exciting—journey of your entire life. You will see to it that you are properly prepared—that your luggage contains everything you require.

In the event you have not yet gotten yourself in the frame of mind to accept this coming experience as a real journey, let's think about it for a few moments.

I always arise rather early in the morning and start my day by getting the newspaper, which I read while enjoying my breakfast. It is quite a walk from our house to our entrance gates. One morning—it was quite cold—I neglected to put on my coat for the walk to get the morning newspaper. I was cold, very much so, but when I opened the door to my study and was greeted by a welcome warmth it was like being lifted from a winter of discomfort to a summer of gladness.

Can we not use this illustration as a parallel to the journey we are about to take?

Let us think of a super conveyance of some kind which is all set to transport us from a land of drudgery, disappointments and a miscellaneous assortment of disconcerting problems. Let it take us into a state of fulfillment, where we no longer wish, but accomplish; where a desire does not mean an empty hope but a mental directive *indicating that* which will add to your happiness and which will be yours as soon as you apply the *principles,* that by then, you will know so well. Can you imagine such a joyous state of affairs? If so, you are ready to prepare to start your journey.

What Kind of Baggage?

So far as material baggage is concerned, you will start your journey with nothing more than the clothing you are wearing at the time. But there will be many things of far greater import than items of wearing apparel.

You have already been told that to accomplish anything you must first know that you *can* accomplish that which you wish to accomplish, and that you will back up that knowledge with an I WILL spirit which gives you the determination to take the steps necessary to attain your objective. This being true, your items of baggage must necessarily include mental attributes. So —right at this point—let us enumerate and evaluate the characteristics necessary to take with us on this journey.

Item Number 1: An I CAN spirit.

There is little sense in trying to do anything unless you know you *can* do it. So, this will be the first item to be packed in your mythical luggage.

"How does one gain an I CAN attitude?" you might ask. It is far simpler than you, at this moment, might think, and *thinking* is all you need to let you realize that you *can* do about anything you really want to do.

The ne'er-do-well can always give you many excuses as to why he does not succeed. Bear in mind, I said excuses—not reasons.

He might tell you he *lacks education*. This is no reason at all. In this day and age with night schools, home-study courses, informative magazines, huge libraries, educational radio and television programs, etc., there is no valid reason why one—at any age—cannot acquire additional education. History teems with cases of men and women who made outstanding marks in life and who started out with little or no education.

One might comment on the *lack of time* to prepare for anything of a self-improvement nature. This, too, is not a reason but an excuse. Most people *waste* more time than they use constructively.

> Work while you work;
> Play while you play.
> That is the way
> To be happy and gay.

This rhyme carried over from childhood days contains a wealth of meaning.

Many people put only half-a-heart into the work they are doing. This means that time drags; the work is not done as well as it might be done. And periods for rest cannot be enjoyed because of the mental attitude toward the lack of quality in the work done.

Lack of time—in most cases—means lack of the proper organization of time.

Lack of experience is an excuse often given for failure to accomplish. This, of course, is seldom true.

A butcher became a draftsman by studying and practicing in his spare time.

A grocery clerk became an inventor by developing ideas in his hobby shop after working hours.

A gardener became a successful salesman by taking on a line of items to sell during his spare time.

As we think about it, we conclude that experience can be had if we determine to gain it.

An I CAN spirit can be quickly developed if you understand

the truth that the only difference between the success and the failure is that one man thinks in terms of I CAN—the other in terms of I CAN'T.

So the first item you pack in your bag will be a consciousness that you *can* do anything you really want to do, the I CAN spirit.

Item Number 2: An I WILL determination.

Although the remainder of this book is devoted to outlining the simple and fascinating steps in developing an I WILL consciousness, we will have to take with us on this journey the components necessary to do so.

The most essential elements in building an I WILL consciousness are:

1. Be Happy.
2. Have an Incentive.
3. Know the Resistances you must Overcome.
4. Have a Plan of Action.
5. Overcome Inertia (Procrastination).
6. Be Ready to Start and Start When Ready.
7. Make Continued Progress.

Be Happy! It is impossible to overestimate the importance of this admonition. When unhappy, the mind has a tendency to lean toward the negative side. We are inclined to question our ability to achieve. We do not feel well physically. The lightest tasks seem difficult and boring.

Happiness generates enthusiasm. When we're happy, we feel good physically. Even while working, time passes quickly and pleasantly.

So, Be Happy! How? You now have one of the best reasons you have ever had. You're starting on a journey which takes you into the land of accomplishment—where you will know that whatsoever you desire is well within the realm of possibility.

You now understand why you are to carefully include a goodly portion of happiness in your luggage.

Have an Incentive. Webster defines Incentive as "That which incites to determination or action."

Even with an I CAN consciousness, you will accomplish nothing unless you have an incentive to do so. The list of incentives is endless. I name a few; you'll think of many more.

To my mind, *love* is the greatest incentive of all. A man deeply devoted to his wife will have an incentive to achieve great things to enable him to be a good provider for his wife and family. He will want his wife to look up to him and admire him as a man of accomplishment.

The unmarried man or woman might want to succeed in properly impressing the prospective mate.

The love for accomplishment is always a potent incentive. The ability to do that which heretofore was thought difficult or impossible is a source of great satisfaction.

The desire to be a leader—to be looked up to and respected is an incentive which will spur the progressive person to action.

To create an estate for future security will give many the incentive needed for accomplishment.

In packing your bags for this journey, take with you just the right incentives that will result in self-improvement and attract to you the better things in life.

Know the Resistances you must Overcome. There are resistances standing between you and the attainment of any objective, otherwise you could have anything you wanted by merely taking possession of it.

Know the resistances which stand between you and the attainment of your objectives. It will then be easy to develop a . . . . .

Plan of Action: Once you know all of the resistances which stand between you and the attainment of your objective, it will be easy to develop a practical plan of action—one which will prepare you to wipe away the obstacles as they appear. And it will be fun to operate such a plan. Seeing the resistances overcome gives you a feeling of self-mastery you can get in no other way.

Overcome Inertia. "Indisposition to motion," is what Webster said in defining Inertia. It could be called laziness—it could be called procrastination. But, whatever we call it, it is a deterrent —a something which holds us stationary, so far as progress is concerned.

A golf enthusiast, no matter how much inertia he might display in his work, will, on his holidays, arise early and, with eagerness, hie himself off to his golf course.

A man with an absorbing hobby, may "soldier" on his job during the day—but will show great activity when dressed in his leisure clothes and at work on a project in his hobby shop.

Overcoming inertia, therefore, appears to be merely a matter of learning to like that which we have to do. This should be easy for those of us who are going on this journey, because everything we do will be a part of a program designed to give us independence, stability, security—and above all, *happiness.*

Be Ready to Start—and Start when Ready! Have you ever tried to push an automobile that was stopped? You can do it, but it takes every ounce of strength you have. After you get it rolling, you have more than ample strength to keep it going. This can apply to human beings. It takes will power to start a job but, once on it, it takes much less energy to keep going.

In my younger days, I frequently went to the beach to paddle around in the water. I never was a good swimmer. After getting into my bathing suit, I would walk across the sand down to the edge of the water and wait until a wave would come in and sprinkle my feet. The sudden feeling of cold caused me to jump back and remain until I mustered up enough courage to try it again. Perhaps the next time I let the water reach my ankles, then again I would scamper back. This kept up for perhaps a half-hour or better and each time I'd get a few inches more of my legs and body wet. But, once wet all over, I would feel warm and enjoy the water.

One day I went to the beach with determination to dive into the first wave and get wet all over at once. I did so and enjoyed every moment of my stay at the ocean.

Each time a new task confronts you, leap right into it. As your work begins to take shape, you'll be proud of yourself for your self-mastery. Friends will be asking you how it is you can accomplish so much. You will smile inwardly as you think: "I've Got a Secret."

Make Continued Progress! What would you think of a surgeon who starts an operation, makes just a portion of the incision, then waits until hours or days later to carry on? You can't imagine such an asinine procedure, can you?

When you start a job, unless you are interrupted for a legitimate reason,—continue until it is completed. It is amazing how much self-respect you will develop as you form such a habit. And remember this! The opinion others have of you is merely a reflection of the opinion you have of yourself.

Laying Out Your Itinerary

I frequently go on lecture tours which, in many cases, cover much of the United States. If time permits, I like to motor and take my wife with me.

Before departing I lay out a complete schedule for the entire trip. It shows where we will stop each night—not only the city but also the hotel or motel. It is astonishing how much such a schedule helps in making the trip more enjoyable. Each morning as we put our bags in the car, instead of wondering how far we should go before lunch and where we would put up for the night, *we knew*. Your itinerary will be a bit more spacious than a typewritten schedule—and it will be far more exciting.

Here is what I want you to do—and do before starting on your next chapter (if you can wait): Go out and get yourself a good sized scrap book. If you are handy at lettering put on the cover the letters: MJITLOAAH. Others will not know what it means, but to you it will signify "My Journey Into The Land of Abundance And Happiness."

Make of this scrap book a thrilling picture book. Paste in pictures of every objective you have listed. If you have a new home on your list, look through the magazines until you find a picture of a home of the type you have in mind. Paste it in your book. In addition to the picture of the home do not be afraid to add "the trimmings." You might want to add pictures of beautiful gardens, a glorious swimming pool, fruit trees, etc.

How about a new car? Get a picture of the very car which would make you most happy and add it to your picture book.

A mink coat, perhaps? All right, clip out a picture of the

model you want and, with your paste jar and brush, make it a part of your itinerary.

Do you enjoy travel? In any hotel lobby you'll find a rack containing information on railroads, airlines, steamships, various countries, etc. Pick out the folders of interest to you, and from them select pictures for your MJITLOAAH. And on and on until your book becomes a visualization of those objectives you have set for yourself.

Do I practice what I preach? I certainly do. Let me tell you of just one instance where my book faithfully worked for me.

Do you remember, during the last world war, when all metals were on the priority list? There was at that time a definite shortage of most everything made of metal.

During that period I decided to equip a hobby shop for myself. I wanted not only a full set of all necessary hand tools, but several of the large power tools. I went to many of the large machinery houses, but they would not even book my order. They said it might be so long before they could fill orders, they didn't want to mislead anyone by listing an order.

I took my visualization book and, from machinery catalogs, clipped pictures of every power tool I wanted. I started making use of this book, as I will soon suggest to you, and seeming miracles began to happen. In no time at all one of the best machinery houses called me telling me one of the machines I wanted could be delivered. I took it. Later the same thing happened again, with a different machine. It was not long before I had every single machine pictured—and more.

As you read this book you will learn that following this procedure is not fantastic, not a relic from the days of black-magic. You will discover to your amazement and pleasure that you are putting into effect the natural laws of attraction, and that to get what you want in life is your rightful heritage.

MJITLOAAH is to be placed conspicuously with your baggage where it will be available for repeated inspection as you travel. In fact, the first thing every morning you are to take this book and run through it, page by page, allowing your eyes to dwell momentarily on each picture. Do this—not with a feeling that you are wishing for those things represented—but that you are actually looking at objectives which are coming into being. Sense a glow of joy radiating from your heart and mind as your eyes fall on each picture.

As you proceed with this book you will better understand *why* I have asked you to lay out this itinerary. But here is one thing I tell you right now which you will readily understand:

Ninety-five percent of all people lean toward the negative side. It is natural for most people, when thinking of something they would like to have, to think in terms of: "Oh! that was not meant for me. I'll never be able to get it." And, with such thoughts we are actually blocking the pathway which would lead to a realization of our desires.

This visualization book, if used as suggested, will train you to automatically think in terms of things you know you *can* have.

• • • • •

Every chapter in this book is important, vitally so. But the success of your journey depends upon how thoroughly you have absorbed the material in the first three.

Before opening the page to the next chapter, do this: Thumb through all of the pages read so far. As you scan each paragraph, ask yourself if you have grasped the full meaning of every thought advanced.

If your eye falls upon a passage which appears a bit vague to you, take the time to re-read that portion again.

I am sure that by now you can sense my sincerity in wanting to make this the greatest experience in your entire life.

As I said before, I am going with you on this journey and before it comes to an end, we will be mighty close friends.

• • • • •

Soon, hand in hand, we'll be heading for our point of departure.

WE'RE READY—LET'S GO!

Once, while on an ocean voyage, a retired department store owner sat in a deck chair next to me. I knew of this man's success. I had seen his fabulous, multi-acre estate. I had an idea of his great fortune.

"When do you think you gained your greatest thrill in life?" I asked. "When you had acquired your first million?" I continued.

With partly closed eyes, and a steady gaze toward the horizon as if in fond reminiscence, he reflected philosophically:

"No, Ben, it was not when I *had* money, but when I first began to *make* money.

"Like most people, I was living from hand to mouth on a fixed salary. Taking care of my wife, my child and keeping up our modest home, took every cent I earned.

"I was not satisfied, however. Other men were doing better than I was, why couldn't I?

"A new item came on the market, one which had considerable merit. It interested me to such an extent I secured the agency for it, and started out getting salesmen to sell it for me.

"After gaining the know-how through experience, I started making money, good money. My earnings, after paying sales commissions and expenses were double what my former salary had been—and were growing steadily.

"It was then that I believe my great thrill was realized.

"I saw myself becoming a better provider. Instead of living in a modest rented house, I could soon make the down payment on a fine new home which would become our own. My wife and young son could wear better clothes. We could set a better table and drive a more beautiful automobile.

"My imagination carried me to the level where I saw us becoming members of the elite country club. It would be simple for us to take our vacations abroad. Our son could attend a good college."

For thirty minutes this man—almost lost in reverie—related the story of his climb from a nobody to a man of affluence. Perhaps his most significant remark was:

"Seeing our dreams come true is one of our greatest sources of satisfaction. Getting things which I longed for, but which I couldn't previously afford, gave me a just cause for rejoicing. The same things now mean little or nothing to me, because there is no effort needed to get them."

It is obvious why I tell this story. My deck companion's huge thrill came when his way of living began to change; when he could see his dreams coming true.

Right now, as you start your journey to success and happiness, you are about to receive your initiation into a new way of life, a condition whereby you virtually possess a wand which will assure you fulfillment of your desires.

If it were possible to reproduce this last paragraph in neon lights, it could not be over-emphasized.

The degree to which you can understandingly accept the thought expressed in the foregoing statement I have italicized for emphasis is in direct proportion to the benefit you will gain from this book.

You are starting on a journey. As to the type vehicle you are boarding, whether a ship, train or plane, call upon your own imagination. But you *are* starting on a journey.

As your means of transportation begins to move forward, you are leaving behind all memories of an unpleasant nature, thoughts of limitation, self-pity, gloom, etc. Memories of your love and friendship for others will go with you, because you will know that from now on you will have the joyous privilege of being able to do for them the things you always had wished you could.

There is a basic reason for the suggestion that you leave all unpleasant memories behind. In the past, whenever a progressive thought would try to enter your consciousness, it might be greeted with so many reasons for failure that it would turn around and hie itself back to the place from which it came. Memories of failure are so conspicuous in one's mind, a positive thought is turned to negative before it has a chance to make itself comfortable.

Recently I went into my hobby shop to design and build a certain type of cabinet I needed. I didn't look around with self-pity and tell myself it can't be done, that there is nothing in the shop resembling the cabinet I wanted. No, I went to the drafting board and made a sketch of the cabinet. I then looked through my lumber pile for the right boards for the job. I accumulated the screws, nails and hardware—and went to work. It was not long before the cabinet was a reality.

From this minute onward, when confronted with a desire of any kind, the intelligence of your free subconscious mind will direct you to think the thoughts and to do the things which will give form to your desire.

• • • • •

As I continue to write this book, my thoughts keep racing back to the years when I was just getting by, when I found great difficulty in maintaining a modest home and partaking in only a few of the better things in life.

During those days, I was exposed to inspirational books. I read volumes of material which held great promise for me if I would but follow the suggestions outlined.

But somehow—I never felt the teachings were intended for me. It always seemed that the big income, the fine home, the shiny, high-powered automobile, all were intended for the other fellow.

It was not until I had passed the so-called middle age of the late forties and had entered into the fifties that I had my first awakening.

"What is the *real* difference between success and failure?" I continued to ask myself. I thought I knew. My answer to this question contained many facts, ranging from inheritance of a fortune to sheer good luck.

It was not until I began an intensive study into the lives of both successes and failures that I made the discovery which changed my life as well as many thousands of others to whom I have given my *magic formula*.

At the time of my revelations, I was living in a modest apartment and had no automobile. I had no savings account and my commercial account never carried more than enough to meet current bills.

Even after making my discovery, it took me a few years to overcome my mental inertia and really begin to take advantage of the discovery I was so certain would elevate me from the depths to vistas of accomplishment, success and glorious happiness.

In my early sixties I moved into an estate in Hillsborough, California, a unique community often referred to as "the millionaire's town." The artistically landscaped grounds of better than an acre and a half attract the attention of artists and photographers. The palatial home, designed by one of the best known architects, is elegantly furnished throughout in French provincial.

Am I bragging? I do not mean to do so. I merely wish to show what a man in his sixties can do. This should be an inspiration to all of you. Those in my age bracket should know that if *I* can do it—*you can too*. The younger generations should understand that they have no valid reason at all to go through life just getting by.

Vital statistics show that the average individual climbs, from a financial point of view, until he reaches the age of fifty. After that he levels off, and soon descends quite rapidly. In other words, if he has not attained security by the age of fifty, the chances are strong that he will end his life as a dependent; either on his family, city, county or state.

In my case I was ten years past the "leveling off point" before I even started to climb. And, I might say, with honest pride, I made greater progress in my sixties than in all of my previous sixty years put together.

I have done nothing that you cannot do. And you can and

will (if you determine) do as well, if not better, than I have done.

You will not have to spend years in groping and trying. The principles being revealed in these pages will enable you to begin your journey enthusiastically upward—now.

It took years to design a safe of the type which readily opens through the use of the letters and numbers contained in the combination.

You can think of the formula being given in this book as the combination to *life's* safe. Applying the combination, you can easily swing open the door, making accessible the realization of life's riches.

● ● ● ● ●

The thinking man when looking at a piece of equipment will not only ask "What will it do?" but "How does it work?" If he knows how it works, he will more readily agree that it will be able to do what the maker claims it will do.

I believe that, while waiting for our journey to really begin, if I give a simple explanation as to why my formula is infallible while thousands of others are not, you will wipe away all semblances of skepticism and doubt, and will proceed on this journey with a spirit never before experienced.

I have said before that 95 per cent of all people lean toward the negative side. They were not born this way, nor did they acquire their negativeness after reaching adulthood. The negative patterns were established in their subconscious minds when they were very young.

When the youngster hesitates "showing off" before strangers, the parents refer to him as being timid. This plants the mental seed of timidity which often stays with him throughout life.

Seeds of failure are implanted in the young child-mind by constantly telling him that money does not grow on trees; daddy isn't rich and had to work hard for every cent he`earns, etc. If the lad leaves a crust of bread on his plate he is told of the thousands of starving people who would love to have that crust, and that the day may come when he will wish that he had it.

The feeling of inadequacy is mentally established through

constantly telling the child "he can't do this and he can't do that."

Have you ever thought you might like to do something of a progressive nature, but were held back by an indescribable something which seemed to whisper: "You had better not try because you might fail!" Do you know where this warning came from? It was merely your subconscious mind projecting into consciousness the impressions gained during your childhood. That's all.

It will now be simple for you to understand why so many people—a large majority, in fact—fail to get good out of the many self-help books. Any desire for self-improvement which may be created through such books is immediately erased by the ingrained negatives which have dwelled within the subconscious mind since childhood.

So thoroughly have you accepted the negative pattern as your way of life, you may find it impossible to see yourself possessing the qualities of material possessions promised by the great authors of such inspirational literature.

• • • • •

If a good painter is called upon to change a building from a dark color to a light color, he most likely would begin by removing all of the old paint. Yes, he could put on several coats of the lighter paint over the dark until he finally obtained the shade he wanted. But, the dark paint would still remain beneath the new paint and probably would, in time, show through.

Removing all of the old paint would give the artisan a good ground on which to begin, and the finished surface would be composed solely of the lighter shades of paint.

The basis of my discovery, earlier referred to, is removing the framework of negative impressions and building up with a consciousness of nothing but positive, constructive pictures. The moment you become one of the five percenters—those with a positive mind—you will find nothing within reason to be impossible of attainment. You will be able to acquire all of the worldly possessions you might desire; you can go when you please and where you please. You will be happy—ideally so.

• • • • •

Have I succeeded in instilling within your mind the conviction that you CAN do things. Do you begin to see yourself acquiring fame or fortune—or both?

Do you like to read success stories? Do they give you a lift or a let down? With the spirit to win, success stories will inspire you "If others can do it, so, too, can I," you think. If you are ruled by your negative subconscious mind, success stories can be depressing because the contrast between your present condition and that of the one in the success story is so great you feel you could never attain such heights and you become discouraged as you conclude that your lot is an unhappy one.

My genuine desire, in unfolding this discovery to you, is to develop within your mind the truth that the day is just around the corner when success stories will be written around *you* and *your* life.

• • • • •

Your journey is under way. It will prove to be the most vivid journey you have ever taken. Your physical eyes still see the scenes to which you have become accustomed, but your mind's eye—which is unlimited as to vision—sees new vistas of opportunity; a new horizon of infinite possibilities for accomplishment.

Earlier I referred to the combination of a safe which contains a series of numbers which, when applied correctly to the lock, opens it.

From this point on, through the entire book, I will give you portions of a complete combination for successful, happy living.

Before this book closes, all of these principles will be assembled in one chapter, bringing together all you need to give the life you want.

Here is the first principle:

You are a success right now! You don't have to wait until

you have money in the bank and your bills all paid before you are a success. You are a success the moment you acquire a success attitude, because with it, you can achieve almost anything you want.

Some might take issue with this statement by saying: "How can I think of myself as being a success? I have no money, no material possessions, and see nothing in the immediate future coming to me."

This might seem like a good question—but let's think about it a moment.

Suppose you have nothing, but all of a sudden receive a check for $1,000,000. You would be elated and would probably proclaim: "I am rich!" But, for the moment, what have you got which you didn't have just before receiving the check?

First of all, your check would have to clear through a bank before you could use any part of it. This means that, for the time, you have no more than you did before. You decide to own a beautiful home. But this takes time. You must select the lot, choose an architect who, incidentally, takes several weeks designing your home. A builder must be selected, and he takes time in building your home.

As you think of it, you must conclude that, should you be given a large sum of money, it would be some time before your circumstances would be changed at all.

With a success attitude, you have all it takes to enable you to *get* what you want. Isn't this much the same as having the large check I referred to? And, doesn't this bear me out in my statement that you are a success right now? You are a success *because* you have the success attitude, with which you can gain what you want, whether it be money, a happy career, or peace of mind.

•　•　•　•　•

Some might say: "You've convinced me that I can succeed if I apply myself, but it will take time. I am tired of living in hope. I would like to see action now."

To this, I refer back to a statement made in the very beginning of this book. Success is *not* a destination, but a journey.

The road ahead appears hard when you see nothing ahead but strife. But, when you get yourself in the frame of mind where you *know* you are a success, your joy will begin at the first indication of accomplishment. You will agree with the man I met on the ocean liner who said: "My thrill did not come when I *had* money, but when I started to *make* money."

You are on your journey. When you packed your luggage you agreed you would not include any of your worries, fears, phobias.

So right now—as you move toward the greener pastures—I want you to take the first steps toward the acquisition of a success attitude.

Every time you think of it, from early morning until time to retire, repeat it silently to yourself: "I Am a Success!" Say it many, many times. As you do so, permit a panorama of thought pictures to cross your mind. Pictures of you doing the things you have always wanted to do, but never felt you could do. See yourself becoming able to do more for your family, your friends, your associates.

Do you like to doodle? Most people do. Well, the next time you have a pencil in your hand and nothing in particular to do with it, instead of making a series of meaningless lines and marks, doodle by making dollar ($) signs. Make a lot of them: big ones, little ones; dark ones, light ones. If your desires run in directions other than money, instead of doodling with the dollar sign, write down: "I Am a Success!" Write it in all sorts of ways. Write it in script. Print it. Make large letters; make small letters. But keep on putting the expression "I Am a Success" down on paper.

Success, as you know, means the achievement of anything of value to you. You can become a success as a singer, musician, painter, writer, lawyer, doctor, architect. So, as you doodle by writing the words "I Am a Success," keep in mind the attainment of that which, to you, would be a success.

• • • • •

And now, as this chapter comes to a close, may I make a

suggestion? It is so vitally important, wouldn't it be a mighty good idea to re-read it before continuing with the next?

In the next chapter you will reach the first station on this memorable journey. Make sure you are building up the right spirit as you travel.

Station 1

HAPPINESS!

Every station you visit on this journey will be a thrilling experience, but none of them will exceed in importance the one you are now reaching.

It will mean much to you because it is your first station on this exciting trip. And, the more you permit yourself to absorb inspiration while in the midst of happiness, the greater will be the good which will come to you at all of the other stations en route.

It *is* possible to achieve a reasonable degree of success in life without being happy. Psychologists can give you many reasons for this. But, success without happiness is not the life for which we are striving.

It might be well, at this point, to reach a common understanding as to what we mean by the word "happiness."

Literally speaking, happiness means to be in a state of luck. The word *hap* means luck. To be happy, means to be lucky.

We will take the broadest meaning of the word, happiness. To us it will mean felicity, beatitude, blessedness and bliss, all fused into a state of well being. Or, to express it more simply, we might say that our major objective is to create a glad-to-be-alive feeling which will give us just cause to be contented with the things we are doing and the thoughts we are thinking. So, in this and following chapters, whenever the word *happiness* is used it will mean *your* interpretation of happiness—that condition which will make *you* extremely glad that you are alive.

It is not possible to overemphasize the importance of developing a happy frame of mind. When unhappy, we approach our work without spirit. Our task appears as drudgery; time passes slowly—and that which we do is not done as well as it might be.

A man came to me, belittling the value of all self-improvement books. He listed all of the better known books and said that he has read all of them, yet had gained nothing tangible from any of them.

This man was extremely unhappy. He was not doing as well by his wife and family as he would like to do. In an attempt to get his wife a few of the modern conveniences, he had over extended his credit and was burdened with a number of monthly payments which left barely enough on which to provide food, shelter and raiment.

I reached in a pocket and removed a bunch of keys. Singling out one particular key, I said:

"Suppose I would hand this key to you and tell you that it unlocked a chest of gold—and that you could help yourself to all you wished. How would you feel?"

"I'd feel great," he responded, not fully understanding what I was driving at.

"If you believe what I had told you about the chest of gold, you wouldn't have to wait until you actually opened it before being happy, would you?" I added.

"No, I guess not. I would be happy because I would *know* what all that the gold would mean to me," he responded, smiling with well-acted sincerity.

"Were you *happy* at the time you were reading any one of the self-improvement books you mentioned?" I inquired.

"How could I be happy when I knew how desperately I needed help?" he criticized petulantly.

Picking up an inspirational book from my library table, I asked another question:

"If I should tell you that this book is the key which will unlock the door to abundance, could you be happy?"

"No, I don't believe so, because I would doubt that it could be true," he argued defensively.

As much to prove a theory as to help this man, I spent three solid hours in helping him to develop a happy attitude while reading a book designed for self-improvement.

I started with a pertinent question:

"While reading a self-help book, does it help your family problem in any way by being in a state of gloom while reading?"

Slightly embarrassed, he admitted that it could not help in any way.

I then explained how much more he could expect from his books if he approached them with a feeling of confidence that they could and would help, and be happy in the thoughts of what he could do for his family once he did start to climb.

In order to establish the fact that success is a state of mind, and that to improve our way of life we must change our thoughts, I related many stories of people who had risen from the depths of despondency to great heights merely through a change of mental attitude.

I handed my visitor a book recognized to be an outstanding self-improvement volume, and said I wanted him to read it, but not until he could do so with a happy mind.

"Before opening the book," I admonished, "relax and meditate for a few moments. Visualize yourself having sufficient means to purchase a new home and fine automobile. Think of the happiness you could give to your wife by being able to send her to fine stores to select a new wardrobe for herself and the children.

"Picture vacation time arriving and, instead of being forced to stay at home, being able to take your family on an extended trip to some exciting place, and being able to stay at the best resorts.

"After you have so mused for a reasonable period," I continued, "think of the book you have as the key which will unlock the door to abundance.

"Instead of reading the book with a 'will it work?' attitude, think of *how* and particularly *when* you will put the principles to work for you."

Converting this man from subconscious rejection to conscious acceptance was not easy. Many times he said he would try, but

that did not satisfy me. To say you will try to do a thing indicates a doubt. One does not *try* to do the things he *knows* he can
do. I did not give up my discourse until I could sense an unmistakable enthusiasm and a definite declaration: "I WILL!"

What happened? A few months later this man showed me a
most interesting plan he had worked out. He had decided to go
into a business of his own, and he was going to do so without
borrowing a cent.

Several of his installment accounts were coming to a close.
He decided that, since he had been able to get along without
that money, he could continue to do so. His plan was to take
the amount he had been paying monthly on his various accounts
and put it into a fund for his new venture.

Also, with the success determination he had developed, he
found ways and means of earning additional money in his spare
time which he could also include.

Now, this man who had formerly failed to get any good from
any self-help book, owns a very successful business and is considered by his wife as an exceptionally good provider.

The key to this man's success was happiness. Until he could
face his future with a happy, optimistic, enthusiastic mind, he
was a failure.

Happiness a *Must!*

Do you now understand why I lay such great stress on happiness? Do you realize why this station we have just entered will
have such an important bearing on our future lives?

"How can *I* be happy?" is a question most frequently asked
by those who have failed. They will follow this question with a
statement containing many, many reasons why they should be
anything but happy.

"Because you do not want to be happy!" I replied to one such
question. I was looked at as though I had not taken the problem
seriously. Then I proceeded to disprove her arguments by pointing out case after case of men and women in circumstances much
less abundant than hers, who were ideally happy.

At one time, I maintained an office on a floor high up in one of New York's familiar skyscrapers. From my window I could plainly see the activity on many of the busy streets.

In New York, there are two uniform dates when people move. Offices are usually leased from May 1st to May 1st. Residences are leased from October 1st to October 1st.

On one occasion—it was October 1st—I peered from my window and, in every direction, one could observe moving vans parked in front of apartment houses. People were moving in—people were moving out. Some were moving from the city into the suburbs—others were moving in from the country to the city.

"Why are these people moving?" I asked myself. Although there undoubtedly were numerous reasons, one answer would be prevalent, I am sure: "to find happiness."

Weary, unhappy city people, might feel that the hustle and bustle of the metropolis is responsible for their morose state of mind. Weary, unhappy suburban people might feel that the lack of activity is responsible for their boredom.

You can not rent happiness! You can not obtain it by changing locations. Unless one takes happiness with him, he will not find it at any destination he might have planned to reach.

Our happiness is not contingent upon people or things, but rather our *attitude* toward people and things. For example: One person might be profoundly happy under a certain set of circumstances. Another might feel he has reason for gloom under identical conditions. As a simple illustration: Mrs. A and Mrs. B may receive gifts of the same kind. Mrs. A's gift appeals to her—and she is happy. Mrs. B's gift—an exact duplicate of Mrs. A's—does not appeal to her, and she is unhappy. You see, it was not the nature of the gift which induced happiness or gloom, it was the attitude of the recipients toward the gifs.

Understanding Unhappiness

If we understand some of the underlying causes of unhappiness, it will be easier for us to bring about happiness through a process of elimination. Here are some of the common causes of unhappiness. You can easily think of more.

Guilty Conscience
Self-Pity
Envy
Selfishness
Timidity
Worry
No Religion

The above will suffice to show you that once we learn the reasons for unhappiness, it will not be difficult to change the cause, bringing about the desired effect: happiness!

Guilty Conscience. When one suffers from a guilty conscience, he consciously or subconsciously feels he is not entitled to happiness. Should he catch himself smiling, he will suddenly stop, feeling that happiness is not for him. There are two principal things one can do when he finds himself held back by a guilty conscience:

1. Correct the condition which is causing the guilty conscience, if at all possible.

2. If there is nothing you can do to make amends for any mistake you have made, then forgive yourself. Cleanse your heart and soul of any ill-will you have been holding against yourself. Declare to yourself that you will profit by your mistakes and prove to be a better citizen and friend as a result of them.

I have made lots of mistakes in my life, many of which cause me to blush as I think of them. But, instead of holding myself back by constantly dwelling on my mistakes, I, through my books, magazine articles, syndicated newspaper column, radio and television programs, have attempted to guide others so they will not make the same mistakes. Through this attitude I can safely say that the world is a better place in which to live, because of realizing and understanding my mistakes.

The right appraisal of the cause of a guilty conscience will enable you to dissolve it, and actually gain happiness as a result of your mistakes.

Self-Pity. The person full of self pity is one really to be pitied. Self-pity is a hang-over from childhood. We can't be happy and pity ourselves at the same time. And, strange as it may seem, the one who indulges in self-pity really does not want to be happy. When one pities himself, he does so to enlist sympathy from those with whom he comes in contact. To appear happy would discourage sympathy. Should this type of person catch himself smiling, he will suddenly change because, after all, we do not sympathize with those who are happy, do we?

Envy. Envy is a destroyer of happiness. If one finds another person living a bit better than he is, with a better home, finer automobile, more clothing, a larger income, etc., he is likely to become sullen—because he does not possess such luxuries.

The mere possession of wealth and luxuries is no assurance of happiness. Some of the most unhappy people I know are rich so far as worldly goods are concerned. On the other hand, I know many who are poor in comparison and are extremely happy.

I am not belittling wealth. I believe everyone is entitled to the luxuries of life as well as the necessities. I am, however, insisting that without the right mental attitude toward worldly possessions, we will fail to find happiness.

"Anticipation is greater than realization," it has been said, and quite truthfully so. This may, at first, seem a bit discouraging if I should imply that once you acquire something it will mean less to you than when you were thinking about getting it.

There is an explanation to this apparently odd mental quirk. Achievement brings one of the greatest satisfactions in life. When we desire something badly enough to turn on our mental power and physical strength and make it a reality, our most profound happiness comes as we see our guided efforts bring our objectives into realization. Naturally we will enjoy that which we created, whether it be a simple project or a giant business. But the master thrill comes as we see our ideas taking form and, one should not consider the attainment of an objective as a destination. It is just a plateau where we pause for happy contemplation of what we have accomplished and to build mental and physical stamina for the next objective, which has been peeping over the horizon as the former one neared completion.

Selfishness. Did you hear the story of the snake which put its tail in its mouth, and ate itself up? As grotesque as this picture is, it bears resemblance to the selfish person.

Selfishness, just as the name implies, means pertaining to self. When one tries to attract everything to himself, although he does not consume himself—as was the case in the ludicrous snake story—he does destroy his happiness. A selfish person is trying to live in direct violation of the fundamental laws of Nature. All Nature is on the giving side. The trees, the flowers, the birds, the sunsets—all are on the giving end. There is an inexhaustible supply of everything. The more we give the more we get. If one is not getting enough in this life he is not giving enough, because all receiving is preceded by giving. Have you ever seen a selfish person who was happy? I haven't.

Timidity. There is a close relationship between timidity and selfishness. Timidity is largely due to self-consciousness or, reversing it, consciousness of self. When we can reach that point where we think of ourselves as contributing toward the happiness of society instead of merely seeking happiness for ourselves, we will be well on the road toward freedom from timidity.

Develop a "you" attitude. Think of people in terms of "what can I do to make you happy?" instead of "what can you do to make me happy?"

"The greatest thing in the world to me is me," said a renowned philosopher. Herein lies the solution to overcoming timidity. If, when with others, you would realize that the greatest thing in the world to that person is himself, and then act accordingly, you'll have no difficulty in overcoming timidity. You will find yourself thinking in terms of making him happy instead of remaining so self-conscious you are afraid to be with others.

Worry. Worry has been described as being the mental pictures we hold of things we do not want, instead of pictures of the things and conditions we do want. Worry and happiness cannot live under the same mental roof. While it is true that worry will destroy happiness, it is also true that, if one will give expression to a sufficient amount of happiness, it will crowd out worry.

We might think of worry as clouds—and happiness as the sunshine. In my plane trips, I have frequently flown above the clouds. Above, the sun was shining brightly. Below, the ground would be dark and dreary due to the clouds. Yes, to those on earth, they knew that, if the clouds were to go, sunshine would prevail. One should likewise understand that, if the clouds of worry should be dispersed, the sunshine of happiness would come through.

A woman once came to me with a long face—drenched with worry. Life was unbearable—according to her story. I asked her to approximate the number of hours she had spent on the cause of her worry. She came up with a rather large figure. I then suggested an experiment she should try. I told her that, for the time being she should lay her worries aside and spend her time in finding a solution for them. She should keep a record of the number of hours she would spend on this constructive side of her picture. Do you know what happened? She later came to me with a perfect solution to her problem and the time taken was only a fraction of the amount of time she had formerly spent in worry. This is something for all of us to keep in mind whenever worry is around to rob us of our happiness.

Religion. Everyone must have a spiritual life and live according to it. A person without religion is like a lost soul wandering about in the wilderness.

With a religion you have a presence constantly guiding you and giving you strength and courage to remain erect at all times, even in face of seeming disaster.

Study the face of the one who sincerely believes in his religion. There is an unmistakable aura of happiness which rises to the realm of ecstasy. Such a person has few problems and none he cannot solve. He faces every condition as a challenge, and knows that with his God all things are possible.

• • • • •

You have reached the first station on your journey—*happiness.*
I have told you of the necessity of being happy, and I have outlined many causes of unhappiness. If past memories are making you unhappy—know that there is only one thing you can do. You cannot relive the past—so decide that every experience you

have had up to now, whether apparently good or bad—has been a stepping stone toward your future.

You have grown through your mistakes because you have learned how to avoid them in the future, and you will do all in your power to help others avoid the same mistakes.

Negative conversation is a destroyer of happiness, so do not participate in it. If, when with others, the conversation turns to negative and sordid subjects, do everything you can to switch it to topics relating to progress.

One of the best ways to fix a thought in your mind is to talk about it.

Talk about happiness to others. Tell them how genuinely happy you are. Motion creates emotion. Talk about your happiness enough and you'll discover how really happy you are. And you'll be broadcasting your happiness to those with whom you come in contact. It will prove contagious. Then their happiness will come back to you, forming a circle of happiness.

Your next station is *Enthusiasm*. And, the happier you are as you approach that station, the greater will be the good which will come to you.

Here is a little—but resultful—experiment. Relax and close your eyes. Say to yourself—ten times—and mean it sincerely: I *Am* Happy.

Station 2

ENTHUSIASM!

Nothing great was ever achieved without enthusiasm," said Emerson, the great essayist. As you soar to the heights, you will prove the correctness of his statement.

To approach any project as a job means that you will do so with a feeling of necessity. You may do the work well enough, but time will drag. To enter into an assignment with a mind of happiness will make the work seem easier and the time will pass more quickly. But, to tackle the job with *enthusiasm* means that you are putting your entire spirit into it. You'll not only do your work well, but will do it a bit better than you have ever done it before. And, the passing of time? Instead of dragging, you will wish there were more hours in which you could work.

Perhaps if you understand a bit as to *why* enthusiasm helps you to make a greater success of any undertaking, you will see the reason for the extreme importance I give to it.

Without becoming technical, I would like to make reference to the subconscious mind, and how it is activated by enthusiasm.

There are two truths I wish to mention at this point which will make my following statements more understandable.

1. *The subconscious mind is the storehouse of memory.*
2. *The subconscious mind has motivating faculties independent of the conscious mind.*

Most thinking can be considered passive. Miscellaneous thoughts will idly flow in and out of consciousness without any particular conscious concern.

47

Enthusiasm, like a catalyst, will accelerate reaction toward a specific objective. It will do so by bringing into use facts stored in the memory and, through its reasoning faculties, use them in shaping and readying conclusions for action.

As an illustration: A man was given a rather unusual assignment. It was something which had never been done before, and since he was accepting it as a job, he approached it with the customary doubts and fears. He failed.

Another man was given the same responsibility, but he accepted it with an entirely different spirit. To him it was a challenge, and he *knew* he could prove capable of bringing it to a successful conclusion. He developed enthusiasm. He succeeded most triumphantly.

Enthusiasm not only develops motive power—but provides guidance.

You have the *will* to achieve, and the direction in which to go to enable you to succeed.

Can Enthusiasm Be Developed?

Is enthusiasm inborn, or is it something which one can consciously develop?

Perhaps this question is unwarranted, because you, right now, have acquired a state of enthusiasm probably greater than you have ever shown before. It has been growing ever since you realized that success is not a destination—but a journey, and that you are on that journey this very moment.

You have become aware that you are master of conditions, and that they will no longer master you. You have not only gained an I CAN consciousness, but you have learned that the greatest satisfaction in life comes from achieving.

Everyone displays enthusiasm at certain times in his life. You might be a baseball fan and suddenly receive passes for an important game. This, in most cases, will bring on feelings of enthusiasm, and it is good that this should happen, because it will add greatly to your enjoyment of the game.

The enthusiasm I am referring to in this chapter is *induced* enthusiasm; a condition which can be consciously developed and maintained. But, bear in mind, it is not a pose; it is genuine and sincere.

Our discussion of enthusiasm in this book was preceded by a chapter on Happiness. We can reverse these subjects and show how enthusiasm will cause happiness.

A famed Hollywood star has created a private museum in which he has relics he has gathered from all parts of the world.

On one occasion, I was a member of a party being escorted through this museum by its owner. My interest was aroused by a certain woman in the party. Her enthusiasm was unbounded. Everything she saw brought forth sincere enthusiasm.

The celebrity paid little attention to others in the party, displaying great interest in this particular woman. There is little need to ask *why*. Merely consult your own feelings and you'll realize that you, yourself, enjoy being in the presence of an enthusiastic person.

An acquaintance of mine is the envy of all who know her. Everyone is always trying to do something for her to make her happy. She is continually receiving gifts. Her name is always conspicuous on guest lists for important affairs. The answer? Can't you guess? Enthusiasm!

She displays so much enthusiasm for everything done for her, people enjoy doing things for her. Her enthusiasm is not measured by the value of the gift or service; it is based upon the thought in back of it.

The Anatomy of Enthusiasm

Enthusiasm, sincere and properly developed, will prove to be a most potent force. It can elevate one in rank, dignity, power, wealth, and character.

Just as a number of petals will combine to make a flower, so, too, will a number of special elements combine to create enthusiasm. Some of them are:

1. Incentive
2. Knowledge that you CAN accomplish

3. Determination
4. Action
5. Self-Appreciation
6. Happiness

Incentive. Without an incentive, there would be little desire for accomplishment and, consequently, no need for enthusiasm.

It takes but a slight stretch of the imagination to bring into view many possible incentives. Probably the greatest incentive is love—love for a mate or love for the one you hope will become your mate.

Do you aspire to own a fine modern home in beautiful surroundings? This would be a good incentive—and one which could easily become a reality with the proper mental backing.

Do you often wish you could head a business of your own? This is well within the realm of possibility, once you acquire the right mental attitude.

Would you like to occupy an important position which would necessitate extensive travel? What would make a better incentive?

You can name many more incentives. Think of that which would mean most to you, and consider it as your incentive.

Knowledge that You Can Accomplish. After you have your incentive, you must reach that state of awareness where you *know* that you can make your incentive a reality.

The ne'er-do-well will name a dozen reasons why he cannot get what he wants in life, but they are not sound reasons, they are merely alibis.

All one needs to do is to compare himself with those who accomplish big things and he'll find only one important difference. The accomplisher is the man who *knows* he can do things. The other doubts his ability to accomplish.

The difference between the go-getter and the failure is neither physical nor educational—it is a matter of consciousness.

This being true, it is necessary only for you to realize that you *can* if you *think you can.* So, after calm reflection, get yourself in an I CAN attitude. Have an incentive and know that you can bring it into being.

Determination. This word is synonymous with the title of this book: I WILL! Although the entire book is dedicated to the premise that an I WILL determination is essential to success, some consideration should be given at this time to the role determination plays in building enthusiasm.

A friend of mine had never visited Hawaii. He had always wanted to go, but invariably would find an excuse for staying at home. He couldn't spare the time, or money. One day something happened which gave him a real incentive for going. He *determined* to take the cruise, and it was not long before he had entirely overcome all his previous resistances and was able to go.

Are you acquainted with any of the "going-to" boys? The world is full of them. They are always *going to* do something.

Twenty years ago, a certain man told me something he was *going to* do. I met him recently, and he hasn't changed a bit. He is still *going to* do that which he talked of so many years ago.

Do you understand why these "going-to" boys never do what they intend doing? It is because of lack of determination.

Perhaps one of the reasons why it is often difficult to build up determination is because of the negatives we imagine as we think about the objective in question. We give so much thought to the work which might be involved, we lose sight of the many advantages of accomplishment.

What Is the Difference Between Work and Play?

Isn't the difference between work and play merely an attitude? Golf is far more strenuous than the work a man does at his office. But golf to him is play—his office routine is work.

A man will do really hard physical labor in his hobby shop— and thoroughly enjoy it; because to him it is *not* work, but play.

In my day I have completed many jobs which, when viewed in retrospect, revealed the vast amount of toil represented in accomplishment. Probably if I had devoted too much thought of the amount of work—prior to starting—I might not have started the jobs at all.

Wouldn't it, therefore, be wise to concentrate on the pleasure we will have upon completion of the project, without dwelling on the work involved?

And, if we could become imbued with the realization of satisfaction which could, and would, come to us as a result of the work, wouldn't it be comparatively simple to build a type of determination which would enable us to carry through?

Action. I often wonder if the English author and critic, William Hazlitt, fully comprehended the significance of his statement: "The more we do, the more we can do; the more busy we are, the more leisure we have."

A bit further, an entire chapter, "Station #4" is devoted to Action, but, to tie in with enthusiasm, it will be briefly touched upon here. Action is *thought* in *motion.* We might have an incentive, we might gain an awareness that we CAN accomplish —and we might even develop the determination to do; but until there is action, it is like the powerful automobile awaiting the pressure on the starter button.

Benjamin Franklin, in his *Poor Richard's Almanac,* referred to procrastination as the thief of time. I take the liberty to change this to: Procrastination is the thief of opportunity. Procrastination merely means postponing action. And why do we postpone action? Because it takes more effort to start a job than it does to keep at it once it is started. We hesitate as we ask ourselves many questions: "What do I do first?", "Where are the things I need for this job?", "Will I be able to do it well?"

This is the manner in which you should approach a task: Decide on what you are going to do and how you will do it— then, without hesitation "dive in." You will have defeated postponement of a victory, and you will be amazed at how well and how fast you will do the job.

Action should not be spasmodic. Once you have started on your objective, your action should be continuous; allowing, of course, adequate time for meals, rest, etc.

Some drivers on the highways will travel at the car's top speed, but stop frequently for drinks and snacks. Other drivers will run along steadily, at lower speeds, and at the end of the day will have covered more ground.

Self-Appreciation. Is it egotistical to appreciate yourself? Not at all. In fact, the world will think no more of you than you think of yourself.

Would you trust the life of a loved one with a doctor who did not think well of himself? Would you place an important legal matter in the hands of a lawyer who did not have faith in himself? Would you have a home designed by an architect who did not look upon himself as being a good architect? The answer to all of these questions, of course, is no.

Self-appreciation results from liking yourself. I am in no wise alluding to narcissism (erotic feeling aroused by one's own body and personality) nor am I, in any way, confusing self-appreciation with egotism (the practice of referring overmuch to oneself).

The feeling I wish to convey as I talk about self-appreciation, is liking yourself for the thoughts you are thinking and the things you are doing.

If you had a child who pleased you greatly, was intelligent, studious, and well-mannered—you would appreciate it and most joyously. Right? This is the type of appreciation you should show toward yourself. But do not confuse *appreciation* with *satisfaction.* The moment you become satisfied with yourself (as you will learn in a later chapter) progress stops. Appreciation, as stated above, is liking yourself for the thoughts you are thinking and the things you are doing.

Happiness. Which came first, the chicken or the egg? Happiness generates enthusiasm, just as enthusiasm will bring about happiness. The previous chapter on happiness should have generated much enthusiasm. What you are now learning about enthusiasm should add greatly to your happiness.

● ● ● ● ●

Roy Spence, a man 33 and of little schooling, came to me for advice. He had no particular skill and was forced to work at jobs not requiring too much education. He could drive quite well, so had been working as a truck driver.

But Roy didn't like this work. He was quite religious, did not drink and did not appreciate the kind of language often used by those with whom he worked. Because he would not join the boys for beer and liquor, nor partake in their off-color story telling, he was continually referred to as a "sissy."

Spence could see no future for himself, except following a life of changing from one ordinary job to another.

What he lacked was enthusiasm for life itself—and particularly the part he might be able to play in life.

"Why don't you go into a business of your own?" I asked.

"What kind of a business could I go into?" He replied, with a doubtful expression on his face. "I have no education, I have no money, nor have I any kind of experience which could apply in a business," he added.

"What do you do during your spare time?" I inquired.

"Nothing much, except work around the garden," he answered as he gazed at my garden through the window in my study.

"Why don't you go into business for yourself taking care of lawns and gardens?" I suggested specifically.

His first expression definitely showed lack of interest. But, as I talked about it, explaining that he could take care of about three gardens of moderate size each day and that he would be his own boss, his eyes began to show a growing interest. It was pointed out that the only investment necessary would be the few dollars he would lay out for a power lawn mower, rakes, spade, etc. He already had most of the tools he would need, he told me.

Touching tactfully on his religious tendencies, I added: "And, Roy, you couldn't feel nearer to God than you would when working among His handiwork."

Enthusiasm began to mount. He realized that a small classified ad in the newspaper was all he needed to be in business. He could even handle the first few gardens in his spare time without having to give up his job until he would have sufficient income to care for his wife and himself.

It might seem that work of this kind offered no particular future; but not to a man with enthusiasm.

Roy Spence got started. He did his work so well his customers were recommending him to their friends, and soon he had a waiting list of those desiring his services. But, this is only the beginning. Spence is now using his evening hours to study landscape gardening with a view to becoming a landscape architect.

This man now realizes that success is not a destination but a journey—and he is growing happier day by day as the golden miles roll by.

● ● ● ● ●

You have arrived at the station: Enthusiasm. This, and the one you just passed: Happiness, are so important I want you to make certain you have fully grasped what they will mean to you in the future.

Please remember, you are not merely reading a book. You are acquiring a new way of life. To compare the you of yesterday with the you of tomorrow would show a contrast comparable to the difference between the caterpillar and the butterfly.

● ● ● ● ●

When you first started reading I WILL, you might have thought you were exposing yourself to something which is possible, but which would require tedious work in order to show results.

How mistaken you were! In fact, every principle discussed is so simple it is difficult to believe it can be effective. Yet, as you ponder over what you have learned, your reasoning judgment will clearly show you how easy it is to change your life from drab monotony to exuberant joy.

And now a word of warning to you as we prepare to move onward to our next station.

Knowledge is of no value unless you make use of it. You have agreed with every word you have read. But merely agreeing that you can be helped through what you are learning is not enough. Make use of the knowledge gained—right now.

You need not wait until you have finished the book—or, I might say, completed this journey, before you begin to use the principles. *Start using them now.* Or a better way to say it is begin *living* the principles. Since, as I said above, you are acquiring a new way of life—it is essential that you begin now in *living* that new way of life.

● ● ● ● ●

Are you enthusiastic? Are you happy? Did you ever believe that you can materially change your life in so short a time?

And, if I might step down to the language of the street I will add: "And, you ain't seen nothin' yet."

HAPPY DISCONTENT!

What a strange name for a station!" you probably thought as you saw it on your itinerary. But, after you alight and mingle with those in and around the station, you will agree that your journey would not be complete without a sojourn here.

A paragraph taken from Elbert Hubbard's *Scrapbook* tells of different types of discontent:

"There are two kinds of discontent in this world: the discontent that works, and the discontent that wrings its hands. The first gets what it wants, and the second loses what it had. There is no cure for the first but success, and there is no cure at all for the second."

It is the first type of discontent with which we will be concerned.

As far as I know, I am the first one to use the expression: "Happy Discontent." I like it. It conveys the exact meaning I have in mind as I refer to discontent.

Happy discontent is that condition whereby you are not satisfied with yourself—or with things, as they are but are happy in the thought that you have within you the power to change yourself—and things—as you like.

Discontent is one of the underlying principles of human progress. It has been the mainspring in the lives of those who have risen to high places in science, industry, business and in our national life.

Phillips Brooks said: "Sad will be the day for any man when

he becomes contented with the thoughts he is thinking and the deeds he is doing—when there is not forever beating at the doors of his soul some great desire to do something larger, which he knows that he was meant and made to do."

Every invention listed in the United States Patent Office is the result of discontent. The inventor, not being satisfied with something as it was, found a way to improve it.

If people were satisfied with horse and buggy transportation, we would not have automobiles, trains and planes.

If people were satisfied with ordinary postal communication, we would not have telephones and telegraph.

Every improvement of any kind reflects discontent with things as they were.

And no man attempts to improve himself mentally, or physically, so long as he is contented with himself as he is.

I have no way of knowing exactly, but I am certain that more than 96 per cent of all people are discontented with themselves as they are, but most of them are of the type that merely wring their hands.

On this journey we have lots of bell ringers—but no hand wringers. We're on this journey because we know there is a new way of life—a glorious way of life—and that it can—and will—be ours. The fact that we have gone this far is an indication of discontent with ourselves and circumstances as they were. As we travel on, and new vistas of glowing opportunities unfold before us, our discontent will become Happy Discontent.

Taking Things for Granted

A great fault with most human beings is that they take themselves for granted. They consciously—or subconsciously—feel that they were intended to be as they are and there is nothing to be done about.

In the thousands of interviews I have had with those who came to me for counsel, the descriptions they give of themselves follow a uniform pattern.

"I am not good at making friends," one will assert in explanation for her loneliness. Question her and you will find she has not made an effort to cultivate friends. She has not learned that to have a friend, you must be a friend.

If this person, instead of accepting a thought that she was destined to be friendless, would become happily discontented with herself as is, she would find how easy it is to surround herself with a circle of friends.

"I am just naturally timid," some will say. To this I reply that no one is naturally timid. Timidity is a mental characteristic we acquire in childhood and, as we grow into adulthood, we retain it because we feel we were intended to be that way. This, of course, is not true.

In my younger days, I was so timid I could not talk to three people at a time without becoming tongue-tied. I was discontented—but, for years was of the hand wringer type. One day I decided to do something about my timidity. Abraham Lincoln played a part in my doing so. I had been reading about his Proclamation of Emancipation.

"Why must I be a slave to this feeling of timidity?" I asked myself, I found no satisfactory answer—so I decided to do something about it. My discontent had changed from passive to active, and I conquered my timidity.

"I am not musical," those who have mastered no instrument will say.

"I am not mechanical," explain those who appear awkward with tools or machines.

"I am not artistic," is the thought expressed by those who exhibit no talent pertaining to design or decoration.

"I have no literary talent," we will hear from those who would like to write, but who never have done so.

And on and on it goes. Men and women attempting to justify their conditions and circumstances accept the thought that "I am this way—or that way," and feel there is little which can be done about it.

There is little we can do to change our general physical characteristics. If we are tall or short, dark or light, we accept ourselves as we are.

Mental characteristics can be changed. And desire for a change is a definite indication that we can change.

Feeling that you can't draw or paint does not mean it is beyond you to become an artist. Liking to be an artist is Nature's way of telling you that you can become an artist. Erase the letter "t" from the word can't and know that you *can* become an artist; apply happy discontent with yourself as you are and, with your newly acquired enthusiasm, you're on your way.

This holds true with any desire you might have. *You are what you think you are.* The moment you change your mental image of yourself—and apply happy discontent to yourself as you are, you will begin going places and doing things.

•   •   •   •   •

John Norman had reached bottom. He had been out of work so long he had not only run into debt, but he had sold and pawned nearly everything he owned which had any value. His telephone had been disconnected and he had been given notice that his gas and electricity would be shut off within a few days if he didn't pay up.

Each morning he would leave home in search of a job and each evening would return wearing the same hopeless expression.

One morning while dressing, he caught a glimpse of himself in a full length mirror in his bedroom. He took a second look, then stepped toward the mirror and began talking to himself.

"You're licked," he said almost aloud. "Who would want a picture of gloom like you in their employ?" he continued with increasing emphasis. His face was a picture of despair. His eyes were listless and the corners of his mouth drooped. It was a face which undoubtedly would arouse sympathy, but not one which would inspire confidence.

John sat down and for several minutes just stared into space while his thoughts raced. Then stepping back to the mirror he actually talked to himself—but this time in an entirely different vein.

"You're *not* licked," he said in contradiction to what he had declared a moment before.

"You're going out right now and find a job for yourself and

prove that you are big enough to provide for your wife and self," he said as a defiant look spread over his face.

Norman, having finished dressing, stepped into the kitchen where his wife was placing the toast and coffee on the table.

"Honey," he started with new enthusiasm, "today I am going to get a job and end our troubles. She was so startled with this sudden change in attitude, she actually spilled some coffee as she poured.

"What's happened?" she asked as she regained her composure.

He explained to her how he had found the answer to his trouble as he gazed on the picture of gloom he saw in his mirror.

"I'm a changed man, m'dear," he exclaimed triumphantly. "With this new spirit I can't lose."

Finishing his scanty breakfast, he gave his wife a warmer-than-usual kiss and was off.

That evening he returned, with a job—and some money in his pocket.

Walking down the street he noticed a "Salesmen Wanted" sign in a window. "This might be it," he thought to himself as he entered for further information.

Door-to-door salesmen were wanted, and commissions were paid at the end of each day. Although this was not exactly what John Norman would have liked—at least he could take advantage of the opportunity.

It is doubtful if many housewives could resist the sincerity of John as he talked about his product. The success attitude he had developed proved contagious—and those with whom he talked seemed to want that which he had to offer.

It would take several pages to give you a full account of all that transpired in the life of John Norman since his eventful awakening. But suffice to say:

John is now a district manager with several salesmen under his direction. His bills are paid and all "hocked" jewelry has been redeemed. He drives a new automobile and, on week-ends with his happy wife, he drives around looking for just the right house on which they might make a down payment.

John Norman had been discontented—decidedly so—but it had been discontent of the hand wringing variety. As soon as he became discontented for allowing himself to descend to such depths—things started to happen.

• • • • •

For many years I have done marriage counselling. I doubt if there are many marital problems which do not come to me for attention.

As varied as these problems are, discontent was paramount in most of them—again, discontent of the hand wringing type.

In each case where I could create a feeling of discontent *with themselves* for having allowed the marriage to crumble, the problem was solved.

On the wall in my office is a motto of mine which reads:

"Making a Success of Your Marriage is Proving Your Leadership in Directing One of the Greatest Institutions on the Face of the Earth."

Invariably I point out that it took no skill or acumen to make a failure of marriage. The successful, happy marriage is the one which reflects leadership.

The moment a husband or wife leaves my office with an expression of "Happy Discontent," the ship of matrimony will get back on an even keel.

Developing "Happy Discontent"

The first thing to do in the development of "Happy Discontent" is to decide what you wish to become discontented about.

In Chapter 2: Mapping Your Journey, you were asked to make up a list of your objectives in three categories: Possessions; Physical Being; Affairs.

Refer back to this list, and think of all of the items not only as objectives—but as opportunities for "Happy Discontent." By now you may wish to revise your list. There may be some you would like to scratch off—others you would like to add. This is fine. Have this list represent your objectives—as of now.

As you view your completed list, you might feel: "Boy, I'll have a real 'mad on' if I get discontented over all of those things."

But don't worry! This is a different type of a discontent than you have ever had before. This is a "Happy Discontent."

And, as I said before: Do not feel that you will have to change all of these conditions at once. In the first place, you couldn't do it and, in the second place, there would be no satisfaction if you could.

In the first chapter you learned that Success is not a destination, but a journey. The real joy in life comes when one is forever moving onward and upward.

If you take the items on your list and re-arrange them in the order of their importance—and start working on them, every day will be exciting as you experience new things.

If you were to get one of the finest stereophonic high-fidelity phonographs and an assortment of records and didn't add to your stock of recordings, you would soon tire of it. You would quickly reach the point where your instrument would not be played. It is the constant flow of new records which keeps the interest alive.

Life is like that. If we could get everything we wanted in one fell swoop; although we might be a bit excited for the time being, we would soon become bored because of the lack of something new.

How About Age?

Many men and women on this journey might agree with everything said so far, but may say: "This is all fine for a younger person, but I am too old to change and make a success of life." Such people will be happy to know that such thinking is unwarranted.

As I write this, I am starting my 71st year. I made greater progress during my 50's than I did in all my first 50 years put together. And I made greater progress in my 60's than I did in my 50's.

And, I haven't stopped yet—nor have I even started to slow down. Although I have acquired a sizable, worthwhile estate, I still have just cause for Happy Discontent. My objective list for possessions yet to come is a long one and it will take some time before they are realized.

"Isn't it too bad you had to wait until you were in the 50's before you began getting the better things in life?" asked a well-wishing friend.

I wouldn't want it any other way than what it is at this moment. Had I acquired when I was 40 what I have today, it would be an old story with me by now. I would be taking everything so much for granted there would be nothing to add to the excitement of life. As it is—each time I realize another objective, new joys come into my life.

On one occasion I spent a week in one of the old, conservative hotels in New York. Among its guests were many retired people of wealth, who lived there permanently.

In the dining room, it was an interesting study to watch the faces of those dining. Men and women, past middle age, would sit there with expressionless faces, showing clearly that they were merely existing—not really living. And many of these people were wealthy. But they had lost the spirit of discontent.

• • • • •

Mary Johnson came to me with a long tale of woe. She had a good husband, but he lacked ambition. His income was sufficient to maintain their very modest home—but they could not afford any of the labor-saving devices such as a washer and dryer and other modern conveniences. The range on which she cooked was old fashioned. She swept the floor with an old carpet sweeper. Although her refrigerator was electric, it dated back to the first ones manufactured.

When Mary would hint to her husband that he could make more money if he would try, she would be told that they were getting along all right as it was. His job seemed quite secure, so he lived day by day with the "let-well-enough-alone" attitude.

Here was a case of a man being held back through contentment.

"There is only one way to change your husband," I explained candidly. "Find some way to make him discontented with his usual way of life."

We looked at each other for a moment without either saying a word. Then I recalled something she had said which gave me an idea. In describing their home she had mentioned that they lived in the suburbs where property was cheap and, although they had a small house, their yard was rather large.

That very day I had seen in the newspaper an ad announcing the sale of power lawn mowers.

"When is your husband's birthday?" I asked.

"It's funny you should ask that," she replied. "It is just a week off."

"If you can afford it," I suggested, "buy one of those power mowers for his birthday."

Sometimes the acquiring of one new gadget may start a chain reaction which will end up with many more. This proved the case with James Johnson.

Friends seeing him proudly mowing his lawn with a put-put mower would comment regarding his being on the progressive side.

Jim began eyeing his automobile. Although it furnished transportation, it looked almost like a museum piece. He did quite a bit of figuring with his income and outgo to see if he could squeeze out enough money each month to make payments on a new car.

He found a way—but his discontent was growing. He realized how much easier his wife's work would be if he could only buy her some of the equipment now found in so many homes.

There was only one answer—more money. In the company where he worked there were many men earning far more money than he was drawing. There were jobs calling for more knowledge than his job required, he knew. But, he also knew that if he really wanted to, he could study and gain the knowledge he would need for a better job.

His spirit of Happy Discontent was bringing results. He got books; he frequented the library; he started associating with men who held some of the better jobs.

It is not necessary to go into further detail regarding the Johnsons. Jim got a better job at nearly twice the income he had formerly earned. They sold their home and bought a better one. And, even with their greatly improved standard of living, they, for the first time, are saving money out of each pay check.

"Neither one of us are contented now," smiled a beaming Mary Johnson as she commented on the transformation which had taken place in their lives. She told of the plans she and Jim had for the future which, when completed, would make their previous achievement fade into insignificance.

"And we'll put it over," Mary added. "With that 'Happy Discontent' you first talked about, we know we can do anything we want to do."

● ● ● ● ●

We have now visited three stations on this fabulous trip; Happiness, Enthusiasm and Happy Discontent. Have you noticed the correlation of these stations?

Has it occurred to you that Happiness, Enthusiasm and Happy Discontent blend together in a most dynamic trinity?

If this journey were to end right now, what you have gained already can change your life so completely you could never appraise its value to you in terms of dollars and cents . . . and there is much more to come.

Station 4

ACTION!

The actions of men are the best interpreters of their thoughts," said the famed English philosopher, John Locke.

The newspapers featured a story about a man who had made a fortune through a very simple idea.

"It's funny, but I had that same idea many years ago," a visitor reflected pensively.

"Why didn't you do something about it?" I asked.

His reply was probably the same as that given by hundreds of thousands of others under the same circumstances—a shrug of the shoulders.

In physics we learn of two different types of energy: *potential* and *kinetic*.

Potential energy is energy existing in possibility, but not in actuality.

Kinetic energy is energy in motion.

We all have potential energy. It becomes kinetic energy when we put it in motion.

Permit me to give you a simple illustration. A bowling ball is placed upon a shelf. You know that if it could roll off it could break anything it might hit—and would undoubtedly put a big dent in the floor. While the ball was motionless, it represented *potential* energy. While falling, it was *kinetic* energy.

Let's refer back to the man who made a fortune through a simple idea and the man who had the same idea previously but did nothing about it. The first man conceived an idea and put it in motion—and reaped a harvest. The second man had an idea and let it lie dormant—bringing nothing but regret.

To dismiss this subject by merely praising the man of action and criticizing the man who failed to act would be decidedly unfair.

The Law of Cause and Effect

Let us, for a moment, think of cause and effect. Inactivity is not a cause, but an effect, and to change the effect we must change the cause.

There are many factors which enter into the cause of inactivity. If we understand these factors, and particularly those which apply to our own case, it will be quite simple to bring about a desired effect by changing the cause.

A few of the reasons for inactivity are:

> Sense of inadequacy
> Lack of time
> Lack of knowledge
> Lack of experience
> Laziness

Sense of Inadequacy. Quite a large percentage of people are held back through a feeling of inadequacy. They have no faith that their thoughts and ideas have value, nor that they are capable of doing anything in a profitable way.

Strange as it may seem, this condition, in most cases, is psychological, the result of a mental impression instilled in the mind while a child.

Thoughtless parents are frequently telling their children the things they *can't* do.

"Get away from that, you'll break it. You don't know anything about it," is a warning often heard from parents correcting their children.

Constant repetition of such statements will have the effect of causing a child to lose confidence in himself and develop a definite feeling of inadequacy.

The individual with this sense of inadequacy might get many

good ideas, but will hesitate to put them into action believing they will not turn out well.

One might ask: "If I have had this failing since childhood how can I overcome it?" This is simple if we will give a thought to the proper procedure.

If you wished to destroy a plant so that it would not continue to grow, you would get down to the roots and remove them, wouldn't you?

A condition of inadequacy is something which started with a thought and has been allowed to keep on growing; a thought "I can't do this—I can't do that."

Knowing this, it is simple to assume that one can erase such thoughts by building on the idea: "I *can* do this—I *can* do that."

We are hearing a great deal today about hypnotism. The long period of misinformation on the subject is gradually being replaced by correct information.

"I could never be hypnotized," many will proudly proclaim—which merely means one of two things. (1) They will not permit themselves to be hypnotized or (2) They lack the power to concentrate on that which is being said by the hypnotist.

Briefly, and simply, hypnotism is the law of suggestion in operation. The hypnotist makes a suggestion and the subject accepts and acts upon it.

Only a small percentage of people are known as hypnotists—although all of us are constantly making suggestions. If the person to whom we make a suggestion has faith in us and our opinions, he most likely will act—consciously or subconsciously —upon the suggestion.

Self-hypnosis is often discussed but little understood. One feels that he must have a super mind in order to actually hypnotize himself. Yet, without realizing it, all of us are constantly being influenced by self-hypnosis.

Everytime you hold a thought: "I know I will fail," you are using a principle of self-hypnosis. You are literally instructing your subconscious mind to guide you in thinking the things and doing the things which will make you fail. When you hold a thought: "I know I can do it," you are—through a principle of self-hypnosis—giving your subconscious mind instructions to guide you to success.

Through the principles of self-hypnosis, you keep alive the impressions imbedded in your subconscious mind as a child.

If you had accepted the thoughts of inadequacy you keep adding to them through constantly thinking: "My ideas have no value; I'm not capable of doing things well."

The principles of self-hypnosis can work for you just as easily as they can work against you. As simple as it may seem, all you have to do is to reverse your thinking. Think in terms of I CAN instead of I Can't, I WILL instead of I Won't.

Try it and see how it works. You read previously that knowledge is of no value unless you use it. Since this is true, begin right now to use that which you have just learned.

Correct the negative condition by replacing it with the positive.

If you have lacked faith in the value of your ideas, begin holding the thought:

"I have a good mind capable of sound, constructive thinking. Thoughts flowing into consciousness are positive, practical thoughts."

Do not expect results by merely saying this once or twice. Remember, you are correcting a condition which has been with you throughout your life.

Since your subconscious mind never sleeps, repeat a statement such as this several times just prior to going to bed, and your subconscious mind will work on it during the night. In the morning after awakening, repeat it many times again. During the day, whenever you think of it—say it again.

It will not be long before you will be noticing a vast change in your thinking. Your feeling of inadequacy will begin to dissolve.

Lack of time. Lack of time is not a reason. It is an excuse.

"You have all the time there is," said Arnold Bennett, and how profoundly right he was.

An old proverb says that time is money, but that is an understatement. Time is more than money. If you have time—you can obtain money. But, though you have great wealth, you cannot buy yourself a minute more time than I have,—or the cat by the fireplace has.

Early Hours Are Golden Hours

"I wish I could take up music," an acquaintance reflected pensively, "but I have no time. When I return home from the office, I haven't enough pep to get interested in practicing and, on week-ends, I feel I should have a bit of recreation so that I will feel fresh for my work on Monday."

I looked into the daily habits of this man. He arose at 7 o'clock, took 20 minutes for shaving, showering and dressing; 20 minutes for breakfast and 20 minutes to reach his bus which took him to his office.

"How about arising at 6:30 and take a half-hour each morning?" I suggested. At first he was extremely unhappy with such a suggestion; feeling I was not a bit interested in the amount of rest he might get. But, he was finally convinced he should at least try the experiment. Now permit me to quote from a statement he later made to me:

"I hit the jack-pot with that idea of yours. Practicing early in the morning was not work at all. It was fun. I began when my mind was fresh and, instead of taking energy from me, it seemed to put me in an alert mood for my work for the day. I have grown so enthusiastic over my music, that, instead of getting up at 6:30 as I did in the beginning, I now find myself at my instrument even earlier."

Budget Your Time

What would happen if a man of limited means did not budget his income? He knows he has certain fixed expenses each month; rent, or payment on his home, food, clothing, travel, insurance. etc. To keep out of financial trouble, he must provide for each of these items from the money he receives monthly.

How many people think of budgeting their time? This is even

more important than budgeting your money. If you lost a dollar, it is possible to regain it; but to regain a lost hour is beyond the realm of possibility. It is gone forever.

Analyze a typical day and see how much more effective it can be. You work eight hours, you sleep eight hours (I believe seven hours are sufficient when one learns how to relax during sleep). This leaves you with eight hours, for what? If you allow three hours for your meals and transportation to and from business, you still have five hours left.

"All work and no play makes Jack a dull boy," we often hear quoted. And it is true. But play, to be effective, should be restful and healthful, as well as enjoyable. Periods of idleness with a mind harassed by thoughts of debts, limited income, and failure to grasp available opportunities cannot be considered as rest. In fact, they add to one's weariness, and often cause despondency.

One man, let's call him Bob Jones, wanted to go into business for himself, but never did so because of lack of time to prepare himself—and lack of capital with which to start.

"What time do you finish your dinner?" I asked.

"About seven," Bob responded, but quickly added: "Do not ask me to use my time after seven for work. I need that time to rest and relax after a tough day at the office."

"Suppose you compromise with yourself," I suggested, "and take the four hours from seven to eleven each Monday, Wednesday and Friday to use in the attainment of your objective. If you could see a great enough reward, could you do that?"

Bob reflected for several seconds then, suddenly and with the air of a martyr, agreed that he could do it.

There were two hurdles for Jones to jump before he could reach his objective. He had to find time to gain the "know how" for the business he had selected, and he had to have money to enter this venture.

Of the two, I concluded his first step should be to acquire the money. With this laid aside, he would have an incentive to work diligently, gaining knowledge and experience, because he would know that he could start a business immediately after he was mentally equipped for it.

Since time had been allotted to this project, it became necessary to find a way to turn this time into money. This proved quite simple.

Bob Jones possessed a likeable personality and was a good conversationalist. It was therefore suggested that he could take up spare-time selling as a means of earning extra money, and to save *all* of it for his coming venture.

The suggestion proved to be a good one. The very first week he earned a bit over $25 in this found time, and it was not long until his commissions were running as high as $100 a week. His newly opened savings account started to grow. The dollars added up to hundreds, and it was not too long until the banker began listing sums in the thousands in his deposit book.

"Nothing succeeds like success," is an axiom of great truth. This applied to the case of Bob Jones.

Becoming so enthused over the success he made with the product he was selling, he obtained an exclusive franchise for a desirable territory. He rented a small office, advertised for salesmen—and was in business.

This man's income mounted so rapidly it would have been easy for him to not only give up his evening work, but to also take off many afternoons for golf or other sports. But not Bob Jones. He had learned the monetary value of his spare hours and knew that to waste them was exactly like throwing away money. He is still spending his after-dinner hours Monday, Wednesday and Friday productively. Instead of exerting his own efforts in selling, however, he takes the extra evening hours and devotes them to working out sales contests and other means of stimulating his rapidly growing business.

Before leaving this case, let Bob tell you in his own words how much pleasure he was sacrificing by giving up his evenings thrice weekly.

"Was I making a sacrifice by devoting three evenings weekly in an attempt to attain my objective? I should say not! After it became apparent that I would soon be in a business of my own, my enthusiasm rose to such an extent I looked forward more to my constructive evenings than the ones I used for rest. Yes sir! *Time is money* and I cashed in on mine instead of letting it vanish into nothingness."

Place a Value on Time

Dollar bills, because they can be held in the hand and exchanged for merchandise and services, have a definite value to us. We wouldn't think of leaving them around where they could be taken or, perhaps, blown away. We guard them. Suppose time was visible and had a tangible value. Would we nonchalantly permit it to leave us without first having exchanged it for something of value to us? No! When given a job, your employer first buys your time, because without time there would be no way to accomplishment. When you go into a store, you know what you are prepared to pay for the items you wish to buy. You would not knowingly pay several times what a piece of merchandise is worth.

Place a value on your time. Consider every hour as being worth so much. In this way you will be able to appraise the value of what you buy with your time.

Am I attempting to make your life so efficient that it will lose its pleasure value? Am I urging that you become a time miser? Am I trying to create a condition whereby the clock will be your enemy? The answer to all of these questions is NO—a thousand times NO!

There is nothing more soul satisfying than to end the day with the knowledge that it has been a day of accomplishment. Such thoughts are conducive to restful relaxation and peaceful sleep.

Play time is just as important as work time. A life should be well balanced. Work a little—rest a little—play a little. This is the magic formula for a happy, successful life. We cannot rest, nor can we play, with benefit—if the mind is filled with thoughts of things which should have, or could have, been done.

Lack of Knowledge. Once a person has overcome his feeling of inadequacy and has learned to organize his time, he will find it easy—and fun—to add to his knowledge. With our well stocked libraries, home-study courses, evening classes for adult education, etc., there is no valid excuse for not being able to add to your knowledge.

If the subject you choose is one in which you are sincerely interested, you will not only find it easy to learn, but it will be enjoyable as well.

Study with regularity. After you have formed a habit of spending certain hours in study, it will become just as natural to you as it is to dress yourself each morning upon arising.

While studying, make haste slowly. As you finish a page, reflect over it for a moment to make certain you fully understand it.

No, as you follow the suggestions so far given in this book, you will not study because you feel you should do so. You'll study because you want to; because you thrill every time a new fact becomes apparent to you.

Lack of Experience. Knowledge is seldom of value until it has been converted into experience. One might learn *how* to sell—but he needs experience in using that knowledge. One could learn *how* to play the piano in just one evening. He could learn about the notes and where they were in the key-board—but he would not be able to *play* the piano. It would take time for him to translate that knowledge into experience.

One gains experience by doing. Just as one may find time for study through organization, in the same way time can be found to gain experience.

It has often been found advisable to take a spare-time job in the field of interest to gain experience.

This chapter—or Station—is intended to spur one to action toward his objective.

Consideration is now being given to causes for inactivity. I will consider one more *cause*—one which I am sure does not apply to you:

Laziness. I never like to see this word used loosely. Laziness, just like inactivity, is not a cause but an effect. And, just like the many causes of inactivity, there are numerous causes of so-called laziness.

One never is lazy while doing things he likes to do. Therefore, to overcome a condition of laziness, *learn to like that which you have to do.*

Constructive Reverie

You are on a journey and are just now passing Station Action.

As you glide joyously on toward your next station, resort to what I might call: Constructive Reverie. Close your eyes and recall your thrill as you reached your first station: Happiness. Bring to mind all you learned while at that station.

Let your musing carry you on to your second station: Enthusiasm. Actually feel your pulse quickening as you discover a new zest for life. You find your problems of yesterday becoming challenges of tomorrow.

As your thoughts carry you on—over the magic miles on through the station you have just passed, Action—think back over your life as it had been, and compare it with what you *know* it can be in the future.

Paraphrasing the words of Demosthenes, I will conclude this chapter with the thought: The three essentials to success are: Action! More Action! Always Action!

Station 5

CONTINUITY

"Each station becomes more fascinating than the ones we have already visited," you might declare.

Feeling this way is the result of a change which is taking place within you. Many will start on this journey with the thought: "It can't do me any harm, and it might do me some good."

But, after you start the journey and find that it is *real*; that it is taking you into a new State of Mind which knows nothing but success and happiness, each new station you reach becomes a glorious experience. This is why the stations, to you, become better and better.

This Station: Continuity, impresses upon our minds that Action should be followed by Continuity of Action.

The famed German poet, Goethe, gave utterance to a great truth when he said: "He who moves not forward goes backward." Nothing stands still. Therefore, those with me on this journey will be impressed with an uncontrollable urge, not only to go into action—but *sustained* action.

There is one point I wish to emphasize. *One should not get himself in the frame of mind where he feels his actions are based on necessity.*

One might spur himself on to do things, but he seldom reaches great heights of accomplishment. His work is not as good as it might be, and he takes no pleasure in doing it.

You are to reach that state of consciousness whereby your actions are based upon a *desire to act* and not upon will power.

Seneca, the Roman philosopher, crystalized this thought in a single sentence when he said: "The greater part of progress is the desire to progress."

This curious mind of mine is always delving into the lives of people to learn why they are as they are. If some person has made an outstanding success I like to learn *how* he differs from the failure. With the failure, I am concerned to know *why* he failed.

In an amazingly large percentage of cases I have found that men have failed because they did not carry through on good intentions.

The man who becomes successful reaches that state because, after he decides upon the course to pursue, does so with consistency.

"Did you have to *drive* yourself?" I asked a man of outstanding achievement.

"*Drive* myself?" he laughed as if greatly amused. "Why, Ben, I never played a game in my life which proved half as exciting. Each day brings new thrills as I see my efforts bearing fruit."

John Dagget, a man of 45, came to me hoping that I could straighten him out so that he could make a success of his life. Up to that point he had failed completely and was rapidly reaching bottom, so far as his spirits were concerned. He wanted to succeed, but seemed to feel that Fate was against him.

In discussing this man's past, I found that since he has reached adulthood, he had "tried his hand" in four separate fields. In each case, however, he had made a change before reaching any goal. In other words, he started action, but there was no continuity to his action. He would start, stop, then through natural law, would go backward.

We discussed each one of these fields of endeavor separately and, through his own admission, he could have succeeded in any one of them—had he followed through.

There Is a Reason for Everything

There is a reason why some people succeed; there is a reason why some people fail.

In this work, I am interested in *reasons* because, if we know why we are as we are, we can, if we wish, do something about it.

Why do so many people start programs which they do not finish? All sorts of expressions are used in describing such people: lazy, shiftless, irresponsible and so on, but mostly, the conclusions are not correct.

One important reason why many people stop before they have attained success is because they entered the field more with a desire to make money than because of an ingrained love for the work.

A young man took up the study of law because of the insistence of his parents. They felt that the legal profession was one of great dignity. They had also heard of some fabulous fees earned by lawyers. They wanted their son to be a lawyer because he would warrant the respect of others and at the same time make a big income.

The son, however, was not at all interested in law. He was interested in commercial activities. He wanted a business where he could deal in tangible commodities. But he allowed his parents to sell him a career as a lawyer. The boy completed his studies, passed the Bar examinations, and opened an office. For three years he struggled, just barely making a living. He had not even married the girl he loved because he felt inadequate to become a good provider.

One of this lawyer's few clients owned and operated a food market but, through age and illness, had to give it up. The young lawyer made a deal with the merchant to take over his business and to pay for it out of profits earned.

The sparks began to fly! This man, at last in a career he liked, made such a success of the business that he paid for it in far less time than he originally estimated it would take, and is now on the road to fortune. Oh, yes, he married the girl.

Whenever anything new comes on the market, you will see a large number of imitators and competitors entering the field. But only a very small percentage of the imitators succeed—and for a very sound reason. In most cases, the pioneers in the field came into it because of their genuine interest. They enjoy everything connected with the work. Imitators and competitors are most frequently attracted to the field because it appears to offer great profit possibilities.

A new service had come on the market; one which had great merit and apparent limitless possibilities. One man in the employ of the company looked at the field as a gold mine and decided to go into the business for himself, instead of merely working for commissions.

He inveigled friends to invest money with him and he established his own company. His business lasted less than a year and when it collapsed, there was a loss of over $37,000. This man is now a handy man at a motel, trying to make a living for himself and wife.

Working According to Plan

Imagine yourself taking a motor trip over roads which were unmarked and which had frequent side roads, also unmarked, running in various directions. You wouldn't get very far, would you? In a very short time, you would give up your trip.

Many times one will fail in his endeavor because of lack of plan. He might have been enthusiastic over the work, but entered into it without being properly prepared.

There are two very important steps you must take before you can lay out a practical plan of action.

First of all, you must know what you want. You must have an objective. You might pause right here, thinking that this is not meant for you, because you do know what you want. But, do you?

It is amazing how few people there are who really know what they do want. They think they know, but pin them down to a definite answer and they're lost.

One must not only have an objective, but he must be specific. If he wants a business of his own, what kind of a business? Manufacturing, wholesale, retail, mail-order? He must see, in his mind's eye, that business so clearly that he can actually imagine himself already in it.

A woman once told me, after hearing my lecture on this subject, that she knew what she wanted: she wanted to be a writer.

"What kind of a writer do you want to be?" I inquired.

She blushed slightly as she admitted she had not given any thought to that. I pointed out to her that there are writers of all types: fiction, science, historical, geographical. There are those who write particularly for children. Some writers specialize in articles for magazines; others will concentrate on newspaper writing and reporting.

With this explanation, she realized that she had only a tiny portion of her objective. She knew the field she would like to enter—but not the specific work she would do in that field.

Are you looking for a better job? Be specific! What kind of job? Picture in your mind a job which would give you so much pleasure you could throw yourself into it entirely and do the work better than it had ever been done before.

And, employers like to engage men and women who know what they want.

In the days when I headed a large business, I often had men come to me for work, telling me that they would take any kind of a job. These applicants did not interest me very much because it was certain they were after an income more than they were after a job.

When a man would tell me he would start with any kind of a job, but one which would lead to a certain predetermined post in the company, I would be interested. I knew I would be engaging a man who would prove himself, through intelligent application, to be a good man.

"There is a certain type of a job I would like to do for you," began one applicant, "and one which I feel I could do quite well."

I was sufficiently interested to ask for details.

This man unfolded a plan for a new department in my business, one which could prove very profitable. He also convinced me that he was qualified to head that department. He got the job.

Here was a case of a man having an objective and being specific about it.

Is your objective a home of your own? Be specific! What size and type of a home would you like to own? Where should it be located?

A man of my acquaintance had been married 26 years and

was still renting the house in which they lived. He and his wife had always wanted a home of their own, but never seemed to be able to acquire one.

This man wanted a home of his own, but that was as far as his imagination would take him.

He was told to be specific, so much so that he could really visualize himself and family living in such a home.

On Sundays, this couple would drive around the neighboring country looking for a desirable location for a home. One day he found the right lot. Both he and his wife felt it was just what they wanted. It so happened the owner was not in need of money and he made an offer for purchase of the property with practically nothing down, and payments spread over a long period of time.

The lot was purchased. They did not avail themselves of the long term payments, however. They became so anxious to really own the ground, the husband worked overtime and put every cent he could spare on his purchase. One day, quite soon, he received a paid-in-full deed for the lot.

While paying for the lot they had been spending their evenings studying house plans. In due time they had in mind the home of their dreams, a home which could adorn their newly acquired real estate.

Banks and Savings Associations will usually lend enough money to build a house, if the lot is desirable and paid for.

Our friends secured the money for their home, and it was not long until they were extending invitations to a house-warming.

This couple had *wanted* a home for the 26 years of their married life. In less than two years from the time they became specific regarding their objective, they moved into a beautiful home of their own.

Consider Your Resistances

There are resistances standing between you and the attainment of any objective. Were this not true, you would be able to take anything which might appeal to you, from a book to a skyscraper.

You have learned that you must have an objective—a specific objective. And, I know, you have accepted my reasoning as to why this is essential.

You must also establish a plan of action which will enable you to attain your objective, but there is an unusually important step you must take before you can even begin to create your plan of action.

You must know every resistance which stands between you and the attainment of your objective so that your plan of action will be such that it will enable you to overcome the resistances.

In my study of success, I have had to study failure in order to learn things to avoid in achieving success.

I found that, in a goodly number of failures, the reason for failure was in not considering the resistances which stood between success and failure. The plans of action were not complete.

On the other hand, if the plan of action is designed with the resistances in mind, when they do appear—and they will—you are prepared for them.

A man might have as an objective a business of his own. What are some of the resistances he may encounter? As a hypothetical case, we will include as resistances: lack of experience, lack of money to enable him to gain knowledge and experience, lack of time to earn extra money needed.

In the words of the Caledonian chieftain, Calgacus; "Whatever is unknown is magnified." This is true regarding the elements which stand between us and our happiness.

If you have an objective which is merely in the form of a wish, the unknown resistances which stand between you and the attainment of such an objective are so magnified you subconsciously feel that it would never be possible for you to be fortunate enough to reach your goal. So you go on, year after year, actually pitying yourself for your lack.

But, with the rules I am now giving you, can't you see how downright simple it will be to achieve your aims? As you write down your resistances, doesn't a feeling of victory steal over you as you sense your mastery over the very conditions which might have been mastering you.

So, after you have a specific objective, take a pencil and

paper and list your resistances. List everything which you think must be considered in your plan of action.

The next two stations you will reach will give a new twist to your resistances. They will be considered as components. But right now we are thinking of the important reason why there is lack of continuity of action on the part of so many who fail to reach their objective—why so many will make a brave start which soon tapers off to nothingness.

After you have listed all of your resistances, you are ready to begin building the plan of action which will enable you to overcome your resistances and attain your objective.

• • • • •

It should now be evident to you that once you start action with happiness, enthusiasm and happy discontent, and do so with a well worked out plan of action, there should be no stopping short of complete triumph.

In the beginning of this chapter you were told that your actions should be based upon a *desire to act,* not forced through the use of will power.

You will now agree with me that once you put yourself on the right track, there will be no letting down. It will take more effort to cause you to relax and rest than it will be to carry on with your work.

Expect Problems

There will never be a time in your life when you will be devoid of problems. And, the bigger you get, the larger will be your problems.

But, with the spirit you are developing on this journey, problems will be accepted as challenges and you'll face them bravely knowing well you are more than able to cope with them.

And, be thankful for your problems. Try for a moment to imagine a life without problems. It would become so boring you wouldn't want to live it.

Would any game be interesting if you were to win every time?

No, it is overcoming obstacles which gives one the thrill of winning.

If, in life, we could have anything we wanted, without effort, we wouldn't want anything.

As a problem arises, give a little prayer of thanks that you are bigger than it is and that it presents an opportunity for further growth, because each time you solve a problem you have grown. You not only correct the situation at hand, but will be able to correct similar ones in the future.

• • • • •

Success is not a destination, but a journey. Isn't this truth becoming more apparent to you as you proceed?

In the earlier days of my life, I had a friend who was a prominent magician. He was generous in teaching me many of his most mysterious tricks. Some of his feats, which seemed almost beyond explanation, when revealed were so simple a child could perform them.

Most of those who have failed to achieve success in life, look at success almost as they would look at a bit of legerdemain— something which can be accomplished only by a select few.

I know I am succeeding in drawing aside the curtain which has been hiding success and showing you in a very simple way that success is not difficult to attain. In fact the most difficult stage in achieving success is to get yourself in the frame of mind where you know it is *not* difficult to succeed.

• • • • •

Up to now on this journey we have been acquiring principles. The next several stations en route will enable us to apply these principles.

Motion creates emotion, says a great philosopher. This is particularly true with all you have been learning in this book.

You were told that you are now acquiring a new way of life. To make this true, you must begin living according to the principles which are being unfolded before you.

You might—and will, I am sure—agree with everything you have read, but until you begin applying the principles to your daily life, they will prove of little value to you.

Day by Day I'm on My Way

"Count that day lost whose slow descending sun views from thy hand no noble action done," are inspiring words from the English botanist, Jacob Bobart.

Habits are so easy to form; both good ones and bad ones. We might have a good resolution to "keep on keeping on" but will be inclined to give in to temptation and neglect our work for a day or two at a time. The more this is done, the easier it is to do and, in time, the enthusiastic effervescence once generated has been dissipated—and away goes our good resolution.

"Day by Day I'm on My Way," is a motto which greets me every morning from the wall of my breakfast room. It has a tendency to cause my thoughts to run in the direction of the things I expect to do that day.

But need I, at this point, caution you regarding your continuity of action?

With the enthusiasm you are developing for your new way of life, you are like a spirited horse at the track awaiting the "Go" signal.

We are about to arrive at the next station. Make certain you have with you all that you just gleaned from the last one.

COMPONENTS!

From a distance, the station we are now approaching might not appear as interesting as many of those just past, but we're in for a happy surprise. What we will gain at this station will prove of great value to us for the rest of our lives.

In physics we learn that all material substances are composed of minute particles, or atoms. Although in this work, we are not going to focus our attention on anything as small as an atom, I do want to point out that any objective one might have represents a composite of numerous elements—components.

Do you know why so comparatively few people attain their objectives? It is because they keep their attention focused on the objective as a unit, without considering the many components required to make up the complete objective.

To illustrate: Mr. Black is a man without means. He works for an average wage and lives very modestly in a small home. His wardrobe is scanty, his car is several years old—and he has no savings.

Mr. Black is acquainted with a Mr. White whose circumstances are quite in contrast to his own. White has an estate of great value: beautiful grounds, a large expensively built home. He employs a housekeeper, maid and gardener. His accumulated wealth permits him to enjoy most of the luxuries of life.

Mr. Black envies Mr. White and wishes that he could trade places with him.

Black's mistake is that he thinks of White's situation as it is and, naturally, the contrast between Black's circumstances and his own is so great, it would take too much of a stretch of the imagination to visualize Black as living under the same conditions.

Let us dissect White's picture and examine its components. In the first place, we discover that White did not step into this situation as it is. No, we find that at one time White lived in exactly the same manner as Black now lives. But White was not satisfied with his lot. He knew that if others could climb to success, he too could do so. He developed *Happy Discontent*.

White started out by using one of the prime principles of success; *find a need—then fill it*. He got the idea for a kitchen gadget which would prove a valuable convenience in every home.

With a little money secured from friends who joined him in his enterprise, White started in business. At first it was not too easy. His company had the usual growing pains of all new ventures. In the beginning White's product was sold locally, then it expanded to where it was sold throughout the state; then to a group of neighboring states—until finally it reached the point of national distribution.

As White grew more successful in his business, he added to his financial strength through carefully chosen investments. Of course, his standard of living kept pace with his progress. He changed homes several times, each time moving to a better one, until he reached the point where he is now.

Looking at the components which comprise White's picture you will not find a single circumstance which is beyond the possibility of Black, or anyone else.

And, White's great satisfaction is not just coming into being, now that he has reached this position. No, to him Success is *not* a Destination—but a Journey.

His enjoyment started the moment he acquired Happy Discontent and decided to do something about it.

• • • • •

Take a reading glass and examine any of the pictures you find in the daily newspaper. You will find that the picture is composed of a multiplicity of dots of varying size.

The situation in which any man finds himself is the result of a chain of experiences. And, to raise himself from his present circumstances to some desired plateau, he will have to plan on the steps he must take to do so.

To add further strength to my theories, let us take another case:

"I'll be glad when my life has ended," moaned a 71 year old man who depended upon his married daughter for every penny he spent.

In his explanation regarding the condition in which he found himself, he commented about a man down the street of his same age, who runs a little business of his own. "He is just lucky, I guess," drawled this man as he gave a sigh of hopelessness.

Here is another case of a man looking at a picture as a whole, instead of breaking it down into its components.

He was told how he could obtain the agency for some good product and build up an income selling it. He did. After he had gotten himself out of the lethargy he had allowed himself to get into, he started to do quite well. He interested a few other "oldsters" in joining with him, and collected an override on each sale they made, all of which added to his income.

Soon this changed individual was able to rent a small apartment of his own and, instead of depending upon his son-in-law for "handouts," actually helped him acquire a home of his own.

This man had formerly spent his time in envying another for the circumstances he was in—without taking into consideration the *components* comprising the picture.

Analyze Your Objective

If you were to take a transcontinental motor trip from, let us say, San Francisco to New York; you wouldn't start out with nothing more than New York in mind. First of all, you would make certain that your transportation would prove adequate. You would see to it that your car was in safe operating condition from motor to tires.

Routes would be considered. Shall you take a northern, central or southern route? If you are a good traveler, you would go so far as to decide on the points of interest worth seeing en route.

In other words, all components comprising the trip would be considered.

Your objective must be considered as a whole comprised of a large number of components.

Occasionally, for pastime, I enjoy assembling jig-saw puzzles. It is interesting to see the small, vari-shaped parts come together, forming an understandable picture.

When we accept the proper attitude toward an objective, it will be like a fascinating game to watch the many components fit together and bring the objectives into being.

Here we might paraphrase our original premise: Success is not a destination, but a journey, and also say: The attainment of our objective is not a destination, but a journey.

Attitude! Attitude! Attitude!

Attitude is everything. Our happiness in life; the success we make—all depends upon the attitude we have toward the future we are facing.

If we wish for a change and cannot accept the right attitude toward the steps which must be taken to make that change, there is little hope.

But, if we can visualize the type of objective which would make us extremely happy, and can see enjoyment in every component making up that objective, we are letting ourselves in for a most thrilling experience.

Under such circumstances, impatience never disturbs you. For after all, what matters if the objective may seem a bit off in the future, if you are enjoying every foot of the way toward that objective?

After hearing a lecture in which I discussed objectives and the elements necessary to complete the objective, a woman approached me with the statement:

"My case is one where your theory will not work," she said. "I want a husband, and I see no way of breaking that objective down into its component parts," she added pertly.

"But you can," I assured her with emphasis. Then I began breaking down her objective into logical steps which can be taken to reach her goal.

Instead of looking for a man, she should first make of herself the kind of a woman a man would be looking for. To do this, one must acquire the various attributes which constitute a magnetic personality. After she builds such a personality, she must expose herself so that she will be "discovered" by the right man. She might do this through her church activities, clubs, and contacts with various public affairs.

It did not take too long before this woman agreed that her objective, just as all others, is made up of many, many components. And, if she retained the enthusiasm she had when she left me, I am sure by now she is the happy wife of a good man.

•   •   •   •   •

Not long ago, while flying across the country, my plane passed over a large housing development. Many hundreds of homes lined the uniform streets. Although the homes varied in design, it was apparent that the entire district was conceived by one group of interests.

"What a gigantic undertaking," I thought as I imagined the millions of dollars invested.

But, as I considered the components, it all resolved itself down to a simple sequence of operations. The idea was first born in the mind of some forward seeing individual. Thoughts were visualized on the drafting board. Property was located; a financial structure was set up and investors interested. Builders were engaged, who, in turn, surrounded themselves with adequate workmen. And on and on it went, step by step, until the picture which met my eyes was completed.

"After one starts toward his objective and sees so many steps ahead, isn't he likely to become discouraged and stop?" I was once asked. In reply, I used an illustration:

"Suppose you started to walk across a very narrow bridge which was suspended over a deep canyon," I said patiently. "Then as you stop and stare down into the space between you and the floor of the canyon, you might become afraid and turn back. Is this not true?"

He admitted it was true, and did not need to wait until I finished the thought. He agreed that if, in crossing the bridge, he would concentrate on reaching the other side, he would have no difficulty in continuing.

One could feel, by what I have just said that, in order to reach his goal, he must drive himself to keep on keeping on. This is not true when you learn to enjoy each stop of the way. Thinking back over the stations you have already visited, you'll know that each step toward your objective will be exciting because you will be motivated by Happiness, Enthusiasm—and a Happy Discontent. You'll look forward to accomplishment because it will be of your own making. You will be proving the statement made by the English poet, W. E. Henley, who said, "I am the master of my fate; I am the captain of my soul."

To Materialize—Visualize

Every accomplishment was first pictures in the imagination. The more visual you can make your objective, the easier it will be to formulate your plan of action which will enable you to attain your objective.

We have been talking about components. You have been shown how every whole is made of parts.

To list the components comprising your objective will aid materially in helping you to visualize exactly what you must do in following through on each step.

Can you imagine an architect designing a building without making use of the drafting board? He puts down on paper every element entering into the construction of the building he has in mind.

He may start out with nothing but a mental picture of the type of a home he wishes to create, but after that through the aid of his instruments—he visualizes each phase of the building.

A man came to me for a mental lift. He had dropped as low as he could get—financially speaking. He was not able to support his wife and son; he was heavily in debt. He actually tried to sell me on the idea that he would do his family a favor if he committed suicide. He had some insurance which was still in effect and which would be of great help to the family. His wife would also be relieved of the expense of taking care of him out of her meager earnings.

"John, suppose someone should tell you that he would present you with a million dollars, if at the end of a year you could show that you have worked yourself out of your present dilemma, what would you do?" I asked this despondent individual.

There was a small desk in the corner of my office. I gave John a pencil and told him to sit down and see what kind of a plan he could work out. I left him alone and went about my business.

In a little more than an hour, John handed me his plan. I was amazed with its practicality and simplicity. I handed it back with the pointed question: "Well, why on earth don't you do it?"

Within five years from that epochal day, John and his family were living in a cozy home he had purchased; he and his family were well dressed, and John had sufficient income to send his son to college.

While John was viewing his circumstances as a whole, the picture looked so black it was discouraging. To rehabilitate himself appeared a hopeless job. But, after John had separated the components and looked at his problem in a step-by-step manner, the climb was easy.

At our previous station, you learned that you should have an objective—and be specific about it—know exactly what it is you wish to accomplish.

Now you are advised to take that objective and break it down into its components.

Write down every step you feel must be taken from your present position to a complete fulfillment of your desire.

Don't be afraid you'll list too many elements. The more steps there are to a given elevation, the easier it is to make the ascent.

Do not forget your enthusiasm as you make this list. Enthusiasm to the mind is like good gasoline is to your car. It causes your mental mechanism to function to better advantage.

Sometimes it is advisable to actually put yourself in the land of make-believe. While making up your list, think of yourself as a great counsellor and that you are laying out the pattern which will guide you to success.

Getting yourself in the right frame of mind will not only add pleasure to your planning, but you'll do much better planning.

A large firm was about to fail. Through blunders in management, business had fallen to a very low degree, and bills payable were mounting so high and so rapidly it looked like only a matter of days before the Sheriff's sign would be on the door.

A young business woman showed courage to tackle this seemingly hopeless job. She went to work and within a year the business was flourishing and most of the past indebtedness had been wiped out.

When asked how she did it, she said, with modesty:

"I started out by making myself believe I was back in college and that the problem facing me was one just given by the professor in economics for me to solve. By handling the whole affair in an impersonal way, I was able to work without any feeling of pressure; therefore my thinking was not tainted with any doubts as to my ability to perform."

A couple I know had wanted to take a trip to Europe. For many years they had this desire, but never reached the point of embarking on a ship.

One fall they heard the component story and immediately understood why they had never succeeded in taking the voyage. This time, without hesitation, they declared they would sail in the spring—and they did.

The first thing the husband did was to visit a travel agency and choose where he would like to take his family—and exactly how much it would cost to do so. This gave him something specific on which to work. Knowing how much money he would need, he was in a position to make plans to acquire this amount prior to sailing.

This man learned—almost to the hour—how much time he would need for the trip. This enabled him to make necessary plans so he could leave his work for that length of time.

There were other components to consider. He wanted to make sure that he and his family would be provided with the right wardrobe, sufficient luggage, and so forth.

After he had thought through on every phase of his worthy

objective, he put his plans into action and, when the date of departure was reached, this fine family was ready.

Many people envy those with magnetic personalities; so much so, in fact, they feel it is beyond hope for them to ever have such personalities themselves.

Again I refer you to the elements which make up a magnetic personality in terms with our present thinking: components.

A magnetic personality is not something which one has or doesn't have. It's a combination of many traits of character: friendliness, generosity, helpfulness, cheerfulness, etc.

Study the one with a magnetic personality. Make a note of every desirable characteristic he possesses. As you examine your list you'll not find a single trait which you cannot acquire.

Do you see how easy it is to develop a likeable personality once you go about it in the right way?

For several years, I conducted classes on Creative Psychology in a Western college. Many of the principles outlined in this book were given to my students. In one of my classes there was a young engineer, who was interested in learning a bit about the mind and how it operated. After having heard a lecture based upon the principle covered in this chapter, the engineer proclaimed:

"This is the first time I have learned of any rules for success which were based on scientific principles," he said with emphasis, and continued: "You have given a formula which, I am sure, will work with the precision one will get when following sound engineering practices."

Throughout my entire life I have always been guided by two key words: why and how? I want to know *why* a thing works and *how* it works.

You will notice throughout this book I have not only given principles, but have explained why and how they work.

Do not treat these principles lightly because they appear so simple. And the best way to fix them in your mind is to make use of them.

Right now, before arriving at the next station which is just ahead of us, take one of your objectives and break it down into its components. List every possible step you must take in attaining your objective.

Arranging Your Components

You have one more important operation in connection with this list. On a railroad timetable, every station is listed in the order in which it will be reached. You are now going to take your list and rearrange each component in the order in which it will be taken.

Write down component number 1—the first step you must take. Then list the component which will naturally follow—and so on until your list of components leads you to your objective.

As an illustration: Your objective is a business of your own. Some of the components on your list might be:

1. Lack of time to acquire money and knowledge
2. Lack of knowledge regarding the business
3. Lack of money
4. Etc. etc. etc.

Here the most important component is the finding of time to enable you to acquire the knowledge. So this must come first.

Your next most important component is gaining knowledge for your new venture. So, this follows the time element. You will use this found time to familiarize yourself with what you must know regarding the matter.

Money comes next on your list. You will use your extra time either in earning extra money, or in interesting outside capital to join you.

Your list, once completed, should enable you to visualize every step you must take, from the *decision* regarding your objective to its *fulfillment*.

• • • • •

As we approached our present station, I intimated that it might not seem too important. Perhaps you agreed with me at the time, but now you are realizing that your journey would be far from complete had you not paused at this station: Components.

ANALYSIS — SYNTHESIS

This journey has become unusually real to me. The men and women with me have become definite personalities. Those who started out with a questioning look on their faces are now becoming radiant as their new way of life unfolds before them.

If my readers are gaining just a portion of the enthusiasm I am acquiring as I develop this material, this will prove to be perhaps the greatest book they have ever purchased.

•   •   •   •   •

We have reached another one of those stations with an odd name—but one we will long remember. We are about to learn the magic formula which makes all accomplishment easy.

Webster defines the word Synthesis as meaning: Composition or combination of parts, elements, etc., so as to form a whole; also, the whole thus formed.

When we think of our objective as a completed whole—that is *synthesis*. At this station we will learn to become *analytical*. For example, instead of thinking of a watch as such (synthesis), we will think of the many, many parts which make it tick (analysis).

A building is built brick by brick; a journey is covered mile by mile; a painting is completed stroke by stroke. Dwelling mentally on a completed whole makes a task seem laborious. Thinking of it in terms of the elements comprising the whole, it becomes simple indeed.

If you intended to build a brick building and kept in mind nothing but a picture of the completed structure, the task would seem so monumental you probably would lack courage to attempt it. But laying a brick is nothing—and putting another brick on top of that brick is just as simple. Yet, if you continue laying brick upon brick, the time will quickly come when a wall is completed.

From this time onward you will begin developing a dual sense of observation. You will think of a thing as a whole then think of it as an assembly of units. This will give you a feeling of mastery you can not gain in any other way.

One time, in connection with my hobby, I took as a project the remodeling of our kitchen. I decided to make it one of the glamour kitchens you see pictured in the popular magazines.

I redesigned the entire room. The existing cabinets were to be taken down; a corner of the room was to be made into a breakfast nook with built-in table and benches. Modern range, refrigerator, dish-washer, etc., were to be installed.

My first work was on the drafting board making necessary plans. This enabled me to list the items of lumber and hardware I would need.

The job was started and, after several weeks, was completed. I was happy with it and the compliments I received added to my satisfaction. But, as I looked back over the multiplicity of things I had to do in completing the job, I am sure that had I realized the work involved before starting the job, I would not have tackled it. Thinking of the work in terms of steps, however, made it easy and enjoyable.

Before taking up writing, I had a friend who was an author. I have seen his manuscripts before they were published. Often they would require a mass of typewritten sheets well over an inch thick.

"That's certainly a tremendous lot of work," I thought as I would see so much written material. I doubted that I would ever be able to accomplish anything which required so much work.

But today, I do not think of a finished book as a mass of pages. I think of it in terms of paragraphs, sentences—even words.

First I take the subject matter of the book and break it down into chapters; each chapter covering one phase of the main subject. This done, I can concentrate my thoughts on one chapter at a time, and it is amazing how quickly the book takes form.

Observation

At this point it will be well to give some thought to the development of the powers of observation.

We all see, but few of us observe. This is quite easy to prove. For instance in your home—or office—you may have several calendars which were given to you. Without looking, name the advertisers whose names appear on the calendars. I think it is safe to assume that in most cases you will not remember; yet those names have been before you since the first of the year.

Recall to mind the color of the houses in your block. In many cases you have lived near those homes for years, yet, when you want to bring to mind details regarding those homes, you have difficulty in doing so.

Whose picture is on a one dollar bill? A five dollar bill? A twenty? You might guess, but you're not sure.

In New York I was talking with a friend of mine regarding an outstanding exhibit. I mentioned the name of the building in which it was located, a large building.

"Where is that building?" he asked. When told, he blushed as he admitted that he had been passing that very building twice daily for several years.

Most people see, but do not observe.

Develop your powers of observation! Form a habit of seeing the elements comprising a whole.

Do you merely see clouds, or the interesting formations and shades, from the fleecy white to the threatening dark grays?

Do you see gardens or the individual flowers which make up the garden?

If looking at a picture, do you merely see the complete picture or are you impressed with the composition, the technique, the coloring?

Nature built us to be observing. If you were to close your eyes, then open them, you would first see a complete picture of everything within range of your observation. That is but a fleeting impression. From that second onward your eyes begin dissecting that picture. They keep looking at smaller areas of that picture until they come down to mere details. Try it and you'll understand what I mean. Close your eyes for a moment, then notice what you see when you open them. Your vision will cover a wide area. But try to keep seeing that entire area. You can't do it. Your eyes will scan that picture until they cover every detail. But, all of this is *seeing*. It is not *observing*.

Seeing is merely accepting pictures of objects which come within range of sight. Observing is recording those pictures in your memory, so that they become a part of your awareness.

Developing your powers of observation will aid you materially with your analysis of the components comprising your objective.

Make it a practice to observe what you see. Select different routes in going to and from your work, and notice what you see en route.

Noticing things stimulates your thinking. You begin understanding why things are as they are, and, in many instances, how they might be bettered.

And as your powers of observation grow, you'll get more out of life. You will not have a tendency to become bored because your mind will be active with interesting thoughts.

Concentration

There is a relationship between observation and concentration, yet there is a distinction between them. They both play an important part in the new life which is unfolding before us.

Observing means to take note of what you see. Concentration is when you marshal your thoughts to remain on a specific object or subject until you have fully developed an idea. At least one person out of every three coming to me for personal consultation will admit that he lacks the ability to concentrate his thoughts. The words "mental concentration" apply to a characteristic of mind he does not possess—at least, according to his own appraisal of himself.

There are cases where people, through physical limitations or psychological complexes, do lack the ability to concentrate, but these are in the minority. The percentage is so small that you, unless a competent doctor has told you otherwise, can consider it does not apply to you.

Powers of mental concentration must be developed. It isn't something which we either have or do not have. This is comforting to know, because, should you believe you are one who cannot concentrate, you can now accept the truth that you can.

Before explaining how to concentrate, it might be well if you would understand why many are not able to do so. Those who have difficulty in concentrating invariably make the statements: "I can't concentrate," if not to others—to themselves.

Making such a statement is exactly the same as instructing the subconscious mind to run rampant and flit from thought to thought.

You will never be able to do anything which you sincerely believe you can't do. This applies to everything. A poor memory is had by the one who *thinks* he can't remember. If you think you can't paint, do not try. If you think you can't master a musical instrument, leave it alone. You'll never write a best seller if you think you can't write. I'm not implying you'll never be able to do these things. But, before you do, your consciousness must change to the point where you know you *can.*

As you know, the subconscious mind has reasoning faculties independent of the conscious mind, but all such reasoning is deductive. Deductive reasoning means reaching conclusions based entirely upon information at hand. As a simple example: One might wish to do a painting job. He has three colors of paint: red, blue and yellow. Reasoning *deductively,* it would be deemed necessary to limit the color of the finished job to one or more of these three colors. *Inductive* reasoning could resort to research which would bring out the fact that, through blending colors, other shades and hues could be obtained.

It might also be pointed out that in its reasoning, the subconscious mind does not even employ logic. It does not ask questions, such as "how?" It might be easier to understand if it were said that the subconscious mind absorbs knowledge by rote, that is, in a mechanical routine way. If you keep repeating the statement: "I Can't Concentrate," your subconscious mind accepts it as fact, and—so long as that thought remains—you simply can't concentrate.

It has often been asked why mind, which is supposed to reflect the perfection of God's handiwork, should accept negative thoughts and, especially, act upon them. A simple explanation is to refer to the dial telephone. The mechanism in the telephone station—which receives your dialing and, without human aid, connects you with another telephone perhaps miles away, is most intricate indeed. If you dial a number correctly, this mechanism goes into operation and the 'phone represented by the number you dialed is called. Should you, through error, dial a wrong number, you are still putting this elaborate equipment into operation, but you become connected with the wrong party.

Your mind operates in a like manner. If you hold a positive thought you get a positive reaction. If you hold a negative thought, you get a negative reaction.

It is now easy to understand that if you are to possess the powers of concentration, you must become aware of the fact that you *can* concentrate. This means that you must begin seeing yourself as possessing the powers of mental concentration.

From this moment onward never think of yourself in any other way except that it is natural for you to concentrate; that, when you direct your thoughts into certain channels, they remain, unmolested by other thoughts, until you have reached a satisfactory conclusion.

There are times when failure to concentrate is due to dislike for the task in hand. The wandering mind can be an escape. The moment such an individual can find something to like about the job he is doing, he has no further trouble in keeping his mind on it.

Laziness could be brought up at this point as a reason for failure to concentrate. However, there is no laziness when one is doing something he truly enjoys doing. So, to do what one likes to do—or to learn to like what he has to do—will eliminate all semblance of laziness.

A feeling of inadequacy may, at times, be responsible for

one's difficulty in concentrating. If he doubts his ability to successfully perform a given task, he may have trouble in keeping his thoughts concentrated on it.

I have noticed that those taking up writing as a career often complain of their inability to concentrate. They tell me it takes them an interminable time to write a story, because their minds wander from one thought to another. What a difference there is after they receive a few acceptance checks. A favorable letter from an editor, accompanied by a check, is like magic. The next story can be written in far less time, and will be much better. You see, a confidence in self becomes established, which makes creative thoughts flow much more fluently.

Exercises for Mental Concentration

I suggest an exercise which will help materially in developing the powers of mental concentration. These exercises—as it will be easy for you to understand—strengthens your *awareness* that you can concentrate.

Place a comfortable chair in a position where you see nothing but a blank wall. Place before you a small stand or table. On this table, lay a book—any book. Your exercise is to relax thoroughly and, for a period of five minutes to keep your mind on nothing but the book. You do not have to look at it and think: "This is a book—this is a book—this is a book." Think about the book in any respect. You can think about the contents, size, color, name, cover design, etc. It will not make any difference how many different phases of the book you think about, so long as you do not let your mind wander from it. If you know anything about the processes of printing, you can visualize the book in its making. You can even think about means of selling the book through stores, mail order, etc.

After you have thought about the book for at least five minutes, take a pencil and paper and write an essay on it based on those things which have come to your mind during your period of contemplation. Save this essay.

The next day take a different object for your essay. Take an apple, orange, or some other fruit. Do the same with this as you did with the book. Think how the fruit grows, the part it plays in nutrition; even the days you gave an apple to the teacher, if you wish. But keep your mind on the object—or something linked to it.

Write an essay based on this last exercise—and save it. Your essays should be about 500 words.

Keep up your exercises daily for at least a week, each day taking a different object and each day writing an essay regarding the chosen object. The reason for keeping the essays is for your own satisfaction. After you have completed your last essay, re-read some of the former ones and note your improvement. You will be amazed to discover how you are growing in every respect. You are developing your powers of observation—as well as your powers of mental concentration—and, as a bonus, you are even improving in your ability to express yourself well.

Divergence from Thoughts Through Association

A lawyer friend of mine admitted to me that he was worried about himself. He told me he could not keep his mind on the case in hand; it kept going from one thought to another. When he first began the practice of law, he was proud of his mental capacities and that he had perfect mastery over mind.

I no sooner had walked into his office before the reason for his trouble was apparent. His desk was a mass of folders, documents and papers of various kinds. It was hard to see the wood of which his desk was made.

"There's your trouble," I exclaimed, pointing a finger toward the top of his desk.

He looked in the direction I indicated and, with a puzzled expression, asked: "Where's the trouble?"

I suggested to this counselor to remove everything from the top of his desk—except the papers pertaining to the case at hand—and I would wager he could concentrate. You know, without my saying so, that the problem ceased to be a problem.

When this lawyer first started his practice, he had nothing

with which to clutter his desk and consequently could concentrate on that which he was doing. As his business grew and he had many files and documents to consider, he permitted his desk to become a depository for all of them. While working on one case, his eyes would fall on the papers of another case and, naturally, thoughts would enter his mind regarding them. This kind of concentration difficulty is called: *divergence from thoughts through association.*

Before beginning work on any creative writing, I like to clear my desk of everything except those things which apply to the subject on which I am writing. Creating such an atmosphere enables me to write better material and in far less time than is normally required.

It is not always possible to free yourself entirely from all interrupting thoughts. The door-bell, the telephone, conversation from others—all are distracting forces. However, the person possessing self-mastery, who has an awareness that he has great powers of mental concentration, will be able to discipline himself to such an extent he will direct his attention right back to the original train of thought without too much loss.

A technique which will prove of help in re-establishing thought after an interruption is to review the last thoughts prior to your interruption. If you are concentrating on writing, and have had your attentions distracted for a moment, re-read the last several lines you have written. In a majority of cases, your mind will fall right back into the former groove.

A common mistake made by many is to create a "disturbance hazard," I mean by this that you become distracted because you expect to be. One may be writing and have several interrupting telephone calls. Disgustedly, he will say something such as: "I'll never be able to keep my mind on this if I am constantly annoyed." Those of us who know anything about the mind and how it operates will understand that, after a few such expressions, the mind is literally shot. It will not be able to focus attention on any subject.

If interrupted several times, instead of creating such a situation, hold the thought that you are happy because you possess

the powers of mental concentration and can—at all times—
return your thoughts to the point where you left off at the time
of the disturbance.

● ● ● ● ●

The station we are soon to leave is Analysis—Synthesis. It
was suggested that, after you can visualize your objective as a
whole, you break it down into its components and analyze
each one.

Doing this not only makes the attainment of the objective
seem simpler to accomplish, but prevents procrastination in
starting.

Considerable time has been devoted to a discussion of observation and concentration. As you go further into this new life
which is unfolding before you, you will be happy that you have
this additional knowledge. It will help you materially in your
analysis of the components which go to make up your objective.

● ● ● ● ●

The next station on this eventful tour has a further bearing on
what you have gained from your last two stops. Be sure you are
ready for it by reviewing and thoroughly understanding everything just presented to you.

Station 8

MAJOR—MINOR

The name of this coming station will remind the baseball fans of the Major and Minor Leagues. And, the ones heeding the instructions here given will gain as much genuine excitement as fans do when watching their favorite team win.

If you were to stop reading right now—and would use the information so far given—you would never need to worry again regarding future security. You could accomplish great things. But my job would not be complete. From this point on, I want to explain to you how to make the most from what you have learned.

The knowledge which you are about to gain has a close relationship to several of the principles already touched upon.

You have agreed with me regarding the advisability of breaking your objective down into its components. It was revealed to you how to consider *resistances* before thinking of your plan of action. You are forming the habit of resorting to *analysis* before *synthesis*.

Now we are going to consider *major* and *minor* objectives. When time permits, I thoroughly enjoy building pieces of furniture in my hobby shop. After cutting and shaping the lumber—and putting it together—there remains a most important operation; staining, varnishing, polishing. The piece of furniture could be used without this latter operation—but it would not be complete, nor would it give the greatest amount of satisfaction.

A young man went to a sage and asked him how to keep a

shot-gun from scattering. "Put in one shot," was this wise man's reply. This is the principle we will use in reaching our objectives.

Major Versus Minor Objectives

Hereafter, think of your objective as your *major* objective. Then break your major objective down into smaller, or *minor* objectives. Your minor objectives will be placed in proper order so that they will follow in sequence from the first minor objective on through to the completion of your major objective.

Remember what you previously learned—your objective (now your major objective) must be specific. You must know exactly what it is you wish to accomplish.

Take your first minor objective and, until it is attained, consider it as your major objective. Lay aside any thoughts you may have regarding your major objective or of any of the succeeding minor objectives. You will be concerned *only* with the first minor objective; as completely as though that is all there is.

Before proceeding with your first objective, consider all of the resistances which stand between you and the attainment of your objective. This will enable you to properly formulate the plan of action which will lift you over the resistances—on to your objective.

After you reach the first minor objective, you are ready to start on your next minor objective which then becomes your major objective.

Let us illustrate with a few examples:

The major objective we will consider is of major magnitude. You would like to invent something; then manufacture it and gain national distribution. Your present financial resources are nil.

When you think of the investment involved in large companies, and the tremendous expense in operating them, this particular objective appears as an impossibility, especially when you are starting out with nothing more than a desire.

But, is it an impossibility? No—not if you consider your desire as a major objective, then break it down into its minors.

In this hypothetical case, you are beginning before you have an invention; so this must, necessarily, become your first minor objective.

(*Please note that, in this first illustration, I am using as a major objective one of monumental proportions because, if it can prove practical in such a case, it will work successfully on all objectives of any size.*)

There are two ways in obtaining an invention: develop it in your own mind, or obtain it from someone else. To make this illustration more comprehensive, let us assume that the desire is to create something yourself, rather than purchase an invention.

You already learned that one of the first principles in building success is to *find a need—then fill it.*

To idlly sit and hold the thought: "I would like to invent something," might not get you anywhere. You must first decide upon what it is you wish to invent. *Find a need—then fill it.*

In one of my books, I tell the story of the man who amassed a fortune with a simple can opener he invented. As some of you may remember, the first can openers were those which you would force into the top of a can and then pump up and down until you were able to remove the lid. The edge of the can would resemble a saw with its many sharp teeth. And many people cut their fingers opening a can, causing, in many cases, the use of naughty words.

One man, instead of swearing when he cut a finger on the sharp edge of a can, asked himself the question: "Why can't a can opener be made which will crimp the tin in instead of out, so that one will not cut his fingers while opening a can?" He found no negative answer to his question, so he invented a safe opener—and made a fortune. He found a need—and he filled it.

"When anything goes wrong, you are face to face with an opportunity for an invention," I told a group of people who were interested in learning *how* to invent. If certain troubles keep showing up in an automobile, the manufacturer will put some creative mind to work discovering an improvement which will eliminate the trouble.

In manufacture, any operation which is slow will be studied for ways and means of speeding up production.

In the home, any duty which is laborious is an opportunity

for an invention. Find an easier, better or more economical way of doing anything, and you've made a definite step toward fame and fortune.

Many make the mistake of feeling that most of the good ideas have already been conceived; that not much is left for the creative mind. What a mistake!

The opportunities for invention are like an inverted pyramid. Each invention gives rise to many more related inventions. Since the development of the first "horseless carriage," thousands of inventions were made to bring forth the automobile we now use.

Look back into the history of radio, from the day of the simple crystal set. Many hundreds of ideas were conceived—and used—to bring it up to its present state. Even television—with its myriad of inventions—would not have come into being had it not been for radio.

In aviation, compare the kite-like plane of the Wright Brothers with the jet liners of today. It would take lots of figuring to add up the millions of inventions represented in the air-liners of today.

And we do not have to refer to major industries—automobile, television, aviation—to prove my point. Think of the evolution of ideas in the home. At one time the ice-box seemed a big step forward, but compare it with the rcfrigerators and freezers of today—and think of the large number of patents involved. The same can be said regarding ranges, clothes washers and dryers, dish-washers. Each item represents a chain of patents.

The point which I am attempting to make is that we will never reach the point of saturation so far as ideas are concerned. Each new one paves the way for a series of improvements.

Become Idea Conscious

Before you can develop a creative mind, you must become aware of the fact that your mind is just as creative as that of anyone else. If you think in terms of: "I never could invent anything," there is no need to try. Nothing will happen because you are virtually instructing your subconscious mind to keep everything of a constructive nature locked up.

Build on the thought: "I have a creative mind. Constructive, practical ideas are constantly flowing into consciousness." Keep this thought in mind and you will become excited as you find inventive ideas calling for your attention.

• • • • •

I have spent some time on the first minor objective in connection with the imaginary major objective we have taken. I did so intentionally, because what has been given so far will be of great help to you throughout your life and because everyone likes to feel he has a creative mind. *Become aware of the fact that you have a creative mind and it will become a reality.*

Your Second Minor. We will now assume that you have attained your first minor objective. You have invented something; let us say a new-type play vehicle for children. You have studied it from all angles and find it to be different from present-day wagons and of far greater interest to the kiddies.

Remember, up to now you have no capital—but you have attained your first minor objective. You have an invention.

It would seem logical to assume that your next minor objective would be arranging for manufacture. Some day you will make it yourself, but it costs money to establish a factory. So, why not think in terms of having it made for you until you build a cash reserve?

Even with an objective as apparently simple as this, you have resistances to overcome. Some of them are: learning of the companies which might be interested in making this item for you; selling them on the merits of the invention; convincing them you are capable of marketing it after it is made.

You find such a concern which will make your vehicle, provided you can acquire sufficient capital to create a market—even if a small one—for it.

Your Third Minor. You have the entire nation—if not the world—as your market. But, advertising and merchandising costs money—lots of it. You, you must remember, are creeping before you walk, and walking before you run. So, in marketing your invention you are going to take the smallest, practical area.

For this illustration, we will assume that you are based in San Francisco. There is what is called the Bay Area, which comprises San Francisco, Oakland, Berkeley, Alameda and a number of small adjacent cities and towns. This will be your initial market. It will be your third minor objective.

By now your sincerity and enthusiasm have attracted the attention of others and you have found it possible to obtain enough money to enable you to "crack" this market. The bulk of the money will go for advertising, since there is no manufacturing expense.

Through the use of well laid plans and mature advertising counsel, you get off to a good start. You gain maximum distribution in this limited area and find yourself ready to expand. This brings you to your next minor objective. This may be an expanded market, taking in Sacramento and down the San Joaquin Valley through Fresno to Bakersfield.

Attaining this objective, you may take as your next one the entire state, then Oregon and Washington. You progress to where you add the states west of the Great Divide. Further objectives take in the territory up to the Mississippi. And on and on you go until you can, at last, see yourself with national distribution.

Of course, you acquired a factory of your own as you progressed. And, you may have even added other items of manufacture in your process of growth.

How About Small Majors?

At clubs and meetings of various kinds, you have envied those who could stand on their feet and, with poise and sound logic, hold an audience spell-bound. You would like to possess such ability yourself, but feel it is one objective you could never attain. You actually become nervous as you try to visualize yourself on a platform.

Apply the Major and Minor theory and you'll see that public speaking is not a talent you are born with, but one which you can easily acquire. I do not mean to use the word "easily" too loosely. If you accept the correct attitude toward public speaking, it will prove easy. If not, you'll continue to quake at the thought of being the focal point in a gathering.

Minor Objective Number One. Your first minor will be to

overcome your tendency toward "stage-fright." You are probably asking yourself: "How can I overcome my timidity?" This question is answered so easily, you will be happily surprised. Let me ask you a question. In a crowd, is there a single person to whom you would hesitate to talk to individually? No? Well, remember, the intelligence of an audience is not multiplied by the number of people present. It is no greater than the intelligence of one person. And, since there is no one person you would hesitate to talk to individually, there is no reason at all why you should fear to talk to a group of them at one time.

Instead of fearing your audience, love it. If you have affection in your heart for those who have come to hear you, there will be warmth in your voice and you will thrill as you sense the genuine affection radiating back to you.

Become conscious of the fact that you enjoy talking to an audience. You like to stand on your feet and give others the benefit of your knowledge and experience.

The "stage-fright" picture most people hold in their minds is the reason they become frightened when exposed to a group.

Hold the picture in your mind of yourself as being at ease when in public, you will quickly be able to mount the dais and give your talk without evidence of nervousness.

Your Second Minor. You must give thought to your delivery. You must not talk too fast, too slow, too loud, too low. You must think of modulation, articulation and expression.

Becoming voice conscious will help you materially in attaining this minor. Watch your voice and you will notice improvement immediately. Read aloud and see how much expression you can give to your voice. Pronounce each word distinctly. Practice with a tape recorder if you have the opportunity. Hear yourself as others hear you.

In your next minor you might give attention to correcting errors in English: gaining experience in the choice of words, adding to your vocabulary, etc.

Preparation of material for a talk will constitute another minor objective, and the last one could be gaining actual experience speaking.

Do you see how much simpler the accomplishment of an objective becomes when you reduce it to minor objectives?

Why Envy Others?

Envy is an indication of doubt. One does not envy another for anything which he knows he can possess.

If you should walk into a large store with a pocket full of money, you wouldn't envy those who might be making purchases of items you would like to have, would you? No! You know that if you wanted such items, it would merely be necessary to step to the counter and make the purchase.

If you envy the man who lives in a better home than yours, it clearly shows your doubt regarding your own ability to acquire such a home for yourself.

If you punch a time-clock in the employ of another and envy the man who employs you, doesn't it show that you doubt that you could ever be an employer yourself?

Instead of envying others for what they have, use the Major-Minor method of obtaining that which you might desire.

In my earlier life, before I learned the principles I am now giving to you, I often resorted to envy and was definitely held back by it. There is a note of finality regarding envy. We have taken for granted that the object of our envy was not meant for us—and we do nothing about it.

Today I cnvy no one. I may admire one for his possessions. If he has something I would like to have, I know the steps I must take to possess it. And if I want it badly enough I begin taking those steps.

To see someone accomplish something of outstanding worth makes me happy. It shows me that such accomplishment is within the realm of possibility and, if another can do it, why can't I?

● ● ● ● ●

You have been given two illustrations of the Major-Minor theory in operation.

Take your list of objectives you have already compiled and think of them one by one. No matter how far away the attainment of any single objective may appear, see how you can bring it close by considering it as a collection of minor objectives.

With what you have acquired from the many stations you have visited, you are equipped to attain any objective you may desire—within reason, of course. If you have lost a leg, an arm, or an eye, it would be beyond the realm of possibility to get another one. But, anything which has been done, is being done, and which others can do; you, if you possess all of your faculties, can also do it.

Our First Plateau

Soon we will reach a most delightful resort where we'll pause. We will pause to permit the full significance of everything we have acquired so far to really catch up with us.

We have gained so much from each station, we must take a period to allow ourselves to fully appreciate the value—the power—the efficacy of that which we have obtained.

Our journey from this point on will take a turn in an entirely different direction.

Up to now we have been receiving the tools which will enable us to make any changes in our lives we desire.

We are about to set up a new standard of living—one so far beyond anything we have already had, there will be no comparison. The more thoroughly we have accepted the principles given at each station, the higher will be our standard of living.

Again I wish to lay great stress upon Happiness and Enthusiasm. Right now, if you have been acquiring from this journey the benefits intended for you, your Happiness and Enthusiasm should be unbounded.

Any semblance of self-pity you may have had has, as if by a miracle, been transformed into justifiable self-confidence.

You feel like a phoenix, arising in youthful fashion from the ashes of past mistakes, wrong living and wrong thinking.

Acquiring the keys to this new life of glorious living has not made you conceited, nor will you ever be. You now see yourself as a better spouse, a better parent, a better citizen—a power in your community.

Your circle of friends will widen now that, through your standing and influence, you can be a better friend.

Station 9

NEW STANDARD OF LIVING

Perhaps in your younger days you might have dreamed of a higher standard of living, but did not believe it was even meant for you.

Now as your vehicle comes to a pause at this station, you may hesitate opening your eyes too wide for fear that you might still be dreaming. On the other hand, there have been so many startling revelations since you began your journey, you are not only receptive toward continued blessings, but are looking forward to them.

Our lives comprise a continuity of habits. Almost everything we do from the moment of arising until we retire at night is based upon habit. You are now on a journey which is taking you into new experiences. You must be prepared to rise up to a new and higher standard of living. By now you should almost feel like Alice in Wonderland as you begin to know that your former dreams can, will—and are coming true.

You now possess the keys to accomplishment. They will open for you doors which heretofore have remained objects of envious wishing.

You have reached a point where you must establish a standard of living which will be in keeping with your new possessions.

The story is told of a farmer who had been able to eke out a mere existence from his farm. He never had money for any of the luxuries of life and often had difficulty in acquiring the necessities.

116

Oil was discovered on this farm and, almost overnight, this once poor farmer became a man of great wealth.

"What are you going to do first, now that you are rich?" asked one of the many news reporters interviewing him.

After thinking for several moments, he replied:

"Well, I guess I will have my wagon painted."

This man's thinking had not raised above the circumstances under which he had been living.

There is another story told about an Oklahoman who had suddenly come into money through the discovery of oil. He had been poor so long, he wanted to display his wealth. He had often heard of the amount of money people of means would spend for meals in restaurants. Here, he thought was an opportunity of showing others that he was well fixed financially.

He went into his usual restaurant and, when asked by the waiter what he would like to have, exclaimed loudly: "Bring me $20 worth of ham and eggs."

A New Standard of Living

Having acquired that which will enable you to obtain what you want in life (money, position, power) to properly enjoy your new possessions, you should begin raising your standard of living. You should now live on a plane which will enable you to enjoy life to its utmost.

In planning a higher standard of living, what are some of the elements which must be taken into consideration? Here are a few of them:

1. *A better home.* Your home should not only provide adequate shelter, but should be such that you will enjoy every minute you spend in it and, when away, will look forward to your return to it. There should be enough bedrooms to care for your present family as well as any possible additions. Think of a guest room with its own bath so that you can make your visitors comfortable. You will undoubtedly have a maid; so, of course, a room with bath will be needed for her.

How about hobbies? Sooner or later, both husband and wife will want some provisions where they can give vent to their hobbies. The wife might like to take up something such as weaving, painting, writing; or she may wish to become a lapidary. See that she has a convenient place where she can enjoy her hobby without having to do a lot of moving and shifting of furnishings. Hubby may want a special room for his power tools or camera equipment. This should be thought of before acquiring a home.

Will there be enough yard space for a swimming pool? Look down over the cities as you're flying and you will see how popular swimming pools are becoming. The time is coming when you will find that your home, without a swimming pool, is as out of date as a house without a garage.

2. *Plan for future security.* Your income will be of your own making. You have all that you need to enable you to establish an income well in keeping with your new standard of living.

The wise individual will not only think of the present, but of the future. Build the type of security which will enable you to maintain your standard of living, even though your income for any reason should be suspended.

Lay out a sound investment program; one where you save with systematic regularity. Money which earns a fair rate of interest, and the interest is compounded, will grow very rapidly. Check the stability and reliability of the institution with whom you invest your funds.

Some people favor annuities and today, many thousands of men and women are enjoying life incomes through annuities.

Income property is generally a good investment. An acquaintance of mine bought an old, run-down home at a low figure. He put it in good shape and rented it, thereby gaining a bit of extra income. He later sold it at a profit and bought a four-family home, which added materially to his income. Going from one real-estate investment to another, he reached a point where he now owns an apartment building of 75 apartments. He has an income which enables him and his family to spend two or three months of every year travelling throughout the world.

3. *Your children's education.* In your new standard of living you will not only want to educate your children, but you will see to it that they get their education from the best sources in the country. It will give you a great source of satisfaction to be

in a position to give to your children a type of education that perhaps you, yourself, were denied in your youth.

I could go on listing many things to be considered: your automobiles, home furnishings, wardrobe, etc., but, since you now understand what I mean by a new standard of living, this will not be necessary.

"Will I Enjoy My New Possessions?"

"After I acquire all those things you're talking about, will I be happy?" is a question often asked. I can tell you in a very simple way how to answer that question.

If there is no selfish motive in back of your desire to own fine things, you can rest assured they will make you happy.

As an example: You might desire to have the finest home in your neighborhood; one which will make all others look cheap in comparison. Yes, you can acquire such a home if you make it an objective—but it soon will fail to make you happy.

In the beginning, it will make you happy to peer through your windows and see Mrs. Jones look admiringly at your magnificent home. But the day will come when Mrs. Jones, or some other neighbor will build a larger or better home—and away goes your pride.

If, on the other hand you designed a home strictly for the convenience and pleasure of your family and yourself, and also one in which you would be better able to entertain your guests and friends, then it would make no difference how many better homes were built, yours would still be functioning as you originally wanted it to function—and you would be happy.

Work—Rest—Play

It might appear that I have created a success formula which will work, provided one works at it without rest or letup. Were this true, I would consider my plan a dismal failure.

One must work to be happy; he must rest to avoid fatigue and must play for diversion. This is the program I have in mind for you.

Comparatively speaking, very few people enjoy their periods

of rest. While attempting to relax, their minds are on the things they should have done, or the things they did and which they should *not* have done. There is such a close tie between mind and body, if the mind is not at rest it is not possible for the body to feel refreshed.

Those of us on this glorious journey who are now living a life of accomplishment will have peace of mind when a rest period comes, because we are contented with the thoughts we are thinking and the things we are doing.

Nature requires periods for the restoration of used energy. Knowing this, we will understand that intervals for rest are not mere indulgences; we are working with Nature in keeping our bodies fit.

For a well balanced life, play is essential. Play, to our days of work and rest, is like dessert after a meal. It offers a change in thinking and doing.

From a psychological standpoint, play is as essential to the mind as rest is to the body.

It has already been pointed out that the subconscious mind has reasoning faculties as well as has the conscious mind. It is a psychological truth that the subconscious mind works best when the conscious mind is either in abeyance or pleasantly occupied.

Many years ago it was my good fortune to be a guest on the yacht of the famous financier, J. Pierpont Morgan. In his personal cabin I observed a solitaire table.

"Do you enjoy playing solitaire, Mr. Morgan?" I asked.

"Yes, I do," he replied. "When confronted by a big problem and the solution does not seem obvious, I get out the cards and play solitaire for a half-hour or so. When I return to the problem, I find I have a new viewpoint, and most frequently reach a conclusion quite quickly."

Adequate periods of play are essential to an active constructive mind.

Right here, it is apropos to say there are a few exceptions to the rule given regarding play. Play is fine—and essential—if of the right kind. Drinking parties, which may take one's mind off of his problems for the time being, do not help the constructive faculties of mind in the least. As a matter of fact, after such a party it takes a period of time before the mind can even function normally.

Card games frequently stimulate one's mind; make it active . . . but to spend hours crouched over a table in a room filled with smoke, is not conducive to mental or physical improvement.

There are many sports which stimulate both mind and body, such as: swimming, rowing, hiking, fishing, golf, tennis, badminton. These, if enjoyed, will prove to be beneficial. Bowling is said to be one sport which exercises every muscle in the body. And it keeps one alert mentally.

In your new standard of living, see to it that you have a balanced program; balanced so far as work, rest and play periods are concerned.

"Work while you work; play while you play.

That is the way to be happy and gay."

This rhyme meant little to me when hearing it as a child. But now it appears to me as sound logic.

The man who does not do his best while at work, never enjoys his rest—because his mind is not at ease. It dwells upon his shortcomings instead of accomplishments.

Learn to relax while resting. This is necessary because when you are tense you are burning energy—when relaxed you are storing energy. A thirty-minute period of rest—while thoroughly relaxed—is far more refreshing than double that amount of time while tense . . .

The word "Recreation" is not fully understood by most people. We think of the word as connoting pleasure or entertainment. It is from the word "recreate" which means to give fresh life to; to create anew.

The purpose, therefore, of recreation is to provide Nature with the opportunity of refreshing one mentally and physically.

"I must take a vacation, I haven't had a rest for years," many will say. To which I say that one does not take a vacation for a rest. In fact, the average person will spend far more energy while on a vacation than he does in his regular occupation. Vacations are taken for a change, not a rest—a change in our thinking and in our doing.

Five-Hour Work Periods

A study made by an eminent psychologist revealed that after spending a period of five hours on any one thing, one will become tired of the work; physically tired—and extremely bored.

Fortunately very seldom will one remain, uninterruptedly, on a single task for a period of five hours. This time is usually broken by lunch and coffee breaks. Even so, after a break or a meal, he returns to the same work.

An industrialist tried putting his men on one occupation in the morning and changing them to another in the afternoon. He found an increase in the amount of work done; the work was done better; there were fewer accidents.

If, in your new standard of living, you are expecting to be your own boss, plan your time so that you will not remain in one groove for too long a time. You will do more work and will be happier while doing it.

In writing, I find that if I stay at my typewriter for a period of five hours without a break, I reach a mental letdown. My thoughts do not flow so freely. For this reason, after four or five hours of writing, I will make a drastic change for a few hours. If I have any outside calls to make, I make them. If the weather is warm, I may take some of my reference books and go out on the patio for a while. Or, I might work on a project in my hobby shop.

When I return to my typewriter, ideas are popping. I will make more progress in an hour than I would in two, had I permitted my mind to weary.

• • • • •

In your new standard of living, you will have to change your attitude toward yourself. If you have been seeing yourself as being subservient to others, you should begin thinking in terms of leadership.

You will develop that presence which alerts people the moment you step into a room. There will be something about you which demands the respect of others. People will look to you for guidance.

Please do not confuse leadership with domineering. A domineering person rules through force and a feeling of fear he generates in the minds of those he controls. They are not happy and will break away from such power at the first opportunity.

A leader develops a following because of the treatment he accords those under his direction. People accept his guidance because they *want* to—not because they are forced to.

In my younger days, I was employed by a man who was a real leader. I enjoyed my work with him to such an extent, I would go as long as three years without taking a vacation.

From this moment on, you are going to see yourself as a leader. Even in your present work, your attitude will be such that your co-workers and associates will have a new respect for you. They will want to cooperate with you to the fullest extent.

Another thought, which is probably unnecessary, is that you never allow conceit to enter your make-up. Your growth in power and humility should run concurrently. I have had the pleasure of meeting and knowing many of the most important people of my time. Invariably, I find that the bigger the man, the more humble he is. Conceit is often noticed in the upstart. He has gained something to which he is not accustomed and it literally goes to his head. He does everything he can to impress his importance on others.

The really big man does not require any effort to impress those with whom he comes in contact. The biblical passage: "By your works ye shall be known," applies to him.

Habit Is a Cable . . .

"Habit is a cable, we weave a thread each day, and at last we cannot break it," said a great philosopher. I'll not go so far as to say a habit cannot be broken; otherwise there would be no need for this book. We are as we are because of the habits we have formed throughout life.

I definitely agree with Confucius who said: "Men's natures are alike; it is their habits that carry them far apart."

The object of this chapter—or, I might say, the reason why we stopped at this station—is to change our habits of living.

We begin living on a higher plane, and to do so, must acquire new habits. A habit is not formed until we can do a thing without thinking about it. As a simple illustration: when you eat, do you give any thought to the way you pick up your food, or to the manner in which you chew it? No! You'll eat and carry on a conversation and hardly realize that you are eating. This is true with everything to which you are accustomed.

When you do something for the first time, you must think through everything you do. In fact, the next several times you do it, you do so consciously. In time, however, you'll reach the point where a habit is formed and you'll perform the operation without conscious direction.

Your advanced standard of living is new to you. For a time it will not be natural for you to think of yourself as a person of affairs. You have new habits to form. Through conscious self-discipline you will begin living as you have decreed that you will live.

It will not be long before new habits will have replaced the old ones. A plainly visible change will take place in your entire being. There will be a spring in your step. Your eyes will cast a sparkle of friendliness blended with a look of steadfast determination.

Your manner of speaking will indicate authority and inspire confidence.

You will develop traits of character which will engender pride and greater love from your family, and esteem from all with whom you come in contact.

•　•　•　•　•

Let me repeat: "Knowledge is of no value until you make use of it." I know you're enthused. I know you are happy. I know you fully agree that this will be the turning point in your life. But, *nothing will happen until you make it happen.*

This is not something you are going to do next month. You're not going to put off your start until next week—or tomorrow. There is only one time that you can start and that time is now—*right now.*

Perhaps one of the best ways to make a start would be to

relax for a few moments, close your eyes and just picture the *new you* which is emerging from the former life of disappointments, starts and stops, and failures.

See yourself according to the plans you are laying out for your new life.

• • • • •

Do you recall your school days when your teacher would give you exercises so that you could fix rules and principles in your mind?

I will suggest an exercise which will seem simple to you—yet the result will be startlingly noticeable.

Before arriving at the next station which is just ahead, repeat to yourself—many times:

"I am happy! I am enthusiastic! I am entering a new life of great accomplishment."

Station 10

A NEW LIFE PATTERN

Here it comes! We are approaching the station which will, perhaps, mean more to us than many of the stations already visited—as glorious as they were.

What we will gain from this station will be more noticeable than anything so far acquired. Wealth does not show, except in your bank book—and in your possessions.

Today attention will be focused on *you*. You are about to acquire the characteristics you admire—and even envy—in others. We now begin the building of a new life pattern—one which will make you outstanding. You will become magnetic. You will gain mastery over self.

The principal difference between the man who is master of himself and the one who is not, is that one has belief in himself, the other has not.

Timidity plays such an important role in the lives of those who lack self-mastery, much time will be devoted during our stay at this station in discussing it.

Yoritomo Tashi, a great Japanese philosopher, defines the source of timidity as: "Mistrust of ourselves, the source of timidity, always springs from lack of confidence in our own strength, and must weaken us by hindering us from giving to our thoughts and their realization the inspiration necessary to exalt them."

Can't you see the individual who lacks self-mastery? And doesn't it become clear to you that, to have self-mastery, it is first necessary to understand yourself and your inherent capabilities so that you can form a new impression of yourself?

126

The word "confidence" was used as that which distinguishes the master from the servant. Even this word must be understood, as it can be negative as well as positive in connotation. A man might have confidence in his lack of self-mastery, just as he can have confidence in his ability to lead, to master, to influence others.

In this work I am going on the assumption that you are at least twice as good as you think you are. I am certain I have been proving it, am proving it—and in the pages to come will continue to prove it.

Probably the greatest difficulty one has to overcome before acquiring self-mastery is to gain a realization that he *can* master himself. Studies made of those who were suffering from timidity or inferiority clearly indicated that the ones so afflicted had no idea they could be otherwise.

An illustration might serve to show how comparatively simple it is for each of us to develop self-mastery.

One day, while strolling through a residential neighborhood, my interest was aroused by two gardens adjacent to each other. The grounds of one house were a riot of color. Gorgeous blossoms of many kinds were contributing their bit to the splendor of the garden. It truly was a sight to behold.

The other garden, if you could refer to it as such, was dismal. The lawn looked mangy; there were scrawny plants scattered here and there, a few of which exhibited undernourished flowers.

This example, perhaps, needs no further comment on my part. Any thinking mind can reason that the only thing which kept the hideous garden from becoming like its neighbor was lack of cultivation. It possessed all the possibilities of the beautiful one.

Personalities are like this. The one possessing self-mastery: self-assurance; that demeanor which commands attention and respect in any gathering—differs only from the shrinking, retiring, fainthearted individual in that his vision has not been focused so that he can see himself as a master instead of a slave.

A magnificent, high-priced automobile was stalled on the highway. Its owner had struggled laboriously for hours in trying to find why it would not go—and how to fix it so it would. After having lost his patience and resorting to a choice selection of profane words, it was found that a simple little wire had become disconnected from the starter button. Only a moment was required to reconnect the wire and the car started off in its usual spirited fashion.

The trouble, which was so tiny, had become so enlarged in the imagination of the owner that he couldn't see the car as anything but a bad one. The entire car, for the time being, was blamed for the small disconnected wire.

Take a large black-board and place a small white dot on it. This dot occupies but an infinitesimal part of the entire board—yet notice how your eyes fall upon it each time you look at the board.

The timid soul is most likely to magnify a personality defect to such a point that it overshadows everything else about himself. He may possess many most valuable traits, but cannot see them due to his fixation on the minor things.

Changing the Mold

In a foundry, all castings would be alike if they did not make changes in the molds. We might think of the subconscious mind as the mold from which our thoughts and actions emanate. If we are not happy with our thoughts and actions, it is very important to change the pattern which has been producing them.

To gain self-mastery it will be necessary literally to create a pattern in our subconscious minds which will give us self-mastery. Just how will we do this? It is much simpler than you might think.

You are as you are, because you see yourself that way. You will not change until your mental pattern is changed.

All your life you probably have held to pictures of negative conditions; timidity or inferiority, perhaps. It may be lack and insecurity you have visualized. Inadequacy could easily stem from childhood and haunt you throughout the years. Any complexes you may have are with you because they form a part of your subconscious mental pattern.

The Turning Point

From this moment onward, you are going to see yourself as you want to be, not as you have been. Since doing this requires a change of habit, it will be accomplished sooner if I break the procedure down into stages—or steps.

Step 1. Begin seeing yourself as you would like to be. Do not resort to wishing. Wishing will get you nowhere. Imagine yourself as being master of yourself. See yourself in the presence of others with perfect poise and self-assurance. Know that others like you because you like them. Think of the satisfaction of being able to help people, to inspire them, gain their admiration and respect. See others accepting your suggestions and counsel, and even seeking your guidance. Do this—not for an hour nor for a day—but until the time arrives when your visions will have become realities.

Step 2. Since it is true that you are what you think you are, it will be necessary that you change the mold pattern of your thinking if you are to change the affects of your thinking.

As a continuation of the visualization as suggested in Step 1, hold the thought: "I am master of my being." Keep this uppermost in mind. Repeat it over and over again: when you awaken in the morning, frequently during the day, and especially before retiring at night.

Even if you at first have difficulty in believing the statement, keep repeating it, because motion creates emotion. In time it will replace the former negative thoughts which have been holding you back.

Step 3. *Do not watch for results.* To do so would indicate that a doubt exists as to the efficacy of these principles. Instead of looking for results, know they are there. If you plant a seed in the ground, you do not see any evidence of the plant for some days to come. But if you properly cultivate and nourish the seed, you know that a plant will materialize. Take this same attitude toward the re-education of your subconscious mind. The negative habit grooves have been there for many years. Your new positive mental pictures will begin working at once, but, like the planted seed, it may require a short period before the transformation becomes apparent. Therefore, continue with your positive pictures, knowing they are being effective. Before you realize it, you will be a reflection of your new trend of thought.

A young man was called upon for a few remarks at a club meeting. His timidity was showing. The uneasy movements of his body, coupled with the tremble in his voice, indicated how ill at ease he was. After the meeting was over, I edged toward him and congratulated him on the words he had spoken. I commented on his ability to express thoughts in words interesting and understandable. I predicted he would some day be a good orator.

Today that man is often called upon, not only by his club, but also by others, to give talks. And his talks are well worth listening to. This change came about entirely due to his new attitude toward himself. Instead of seeing himself as a timid, shrinking individual while on his feet, he began visualizing himself as an interesting public speaker.

Doesn't this seem to prove the proverb of the English philosophical writer, Herbert Spencer, who said: "It is the mind that maketh good or ill, that maketh wretch or happy, rich or poor."

Mastery of Habits

In your new life pattern you will make a declaration of emancipation from slavery of habit. You will decree that you will do only those things you want to do, not things you feel compelled to do through power of habit.

If I step on any of your toes, I am also stepping on my own toes as I was in days gone by. I had many bad habits which I put under control in exactly the same manner as I will outline to you.

Here is a truth which will help you in mastering habit. *Man is not a body with a mind. He is a mind with a body.* Man is mind. His body is merely a utility for his mind. The only basic difference between people is their minds. Our bodies are all composed of the same elements. We all require air, nourishment, rest.

When you realize that *you are mind* and that your body is merely your body to dictate to you what you shall and shall not do.

Most People Are Liars

This sounds a bit harsh, and is harsh unless I modify it to mean that most of us are constantly lying to *ourselves*. If the average individual makes a promise to another he will keep it. He knows he would feel guilty every time he saw that person if he should break his promise.

But our conscience seldom bothers us when we break the promises we make to *ourselves*. Yet it should really bother us *more,* because we have to live with ourselves—not with those we make promises to.

As an illustration: One might stay up night after night watching the late television programs. In the morning he has difficulty opening his eyes. Bravely he declared: "Tonight I am going to bed early." That evening, in the t.v. log, he notices a program he simply must see. He does—and breaks a promise.

Perhaps on pay-day, after making his many payments, he finds himself down to his last few dollars. Disgustedly he proclaims: "Next month I'm going to start to save money." The next month he has the same obligations—and temptations—and his money goes. He has broken another promise.

We are constantly promising ourselves that we'll do this, or not do that—but do not keep the promises made.

Being truthful with yourself is not as easy as it seems. Many years ago I made myself the promise that in the future I would keep the promises I would make to myself. It took a terrific amount of will-power to keep that promise. Probably I did not succeed 100 per cent, but making myself always conscious of the promise, I did keep it in a large percentage of cases.

If I say to myself: "Tomorrow morning I'm going to tackle that particular job I have been dreading." In the morning there will be a tendency to lay it aside for some other time. Excuses will come to mind which would seem to justify a postponement. But, I am aware of the promise I made myself, and I start the job. Naturally, after it is done, I am proud of myself and unusually happy that I did not give in to impulse.

Many times we can control, or overcome, habits through the use of reason.

I never was a drunkard. I could count the number of times I have been intoxicated on the fingers of one hand. But I was developing into a constant drinker. During the day, while writing, I had formed a habit of going to my liquor closet many times daily for a sip. A condition of this kind, unless curbed, will never get better; it always gets worse.

A paragraph in a book called: "What About Alcohol?" caused me to give up alcoholic beverages entirely. In this book, Dr. Emil Bogen said: "A person who drinks alcoholic liquors may not know when he is tired as quickly as one who does not drink. Therefore he often feels that he is not tired, and thinks that he is working faster and longer than he really is. Because of this mental effect, a man may feel refreshed and work a little faster after taking a drink, yet he tires more quickly than if he had not been drinking. No matter which muscles are used, or in what form they are tested, the use of alcohol leads to the slowing and weakening of their action."

In my hobby shop are many power tools, any one of which could be dangerous if carelessly used. The paragraph above made me realize that when working—after having taken a drink—how easy it would be for me to lose a finger or two, due to the slowing down process of alcohol. I also reasoned that the amount of money spent each week for alcoholic beverages would buy many more fine tools for my shop, and I agreed with myself that I would get more satisfaction from the tools than from the "dark-brown" taste I had been awakening with each morning.

I stopped drinking and it has been many, many years since I have taken a drop of liquor of any kind.

Yes, I have had a great many temptations. At banquets I have been urged to take a glass of champagne, but I had promised myself I would take no more drinks and, sometimes with effort, I kept my promise.

I couldn't tell you how many thousands of cigarettes I have smoked throughout my life. I started when just a youth, and—

before I stopped smoking—had developed the habit up to a point where I was smoking about 50 cigarettes a day.

I would try to justify my habit. I would say that I gained relaxation through them; that I could sit back for a while and fill my lungs with smoke and that it would help me with my work. I even went so far as to tell people that I did not want to quit because I got so much pleasure from smoking. But this was not really true, even if I had accepted it as truth.

When any habit has taken hold of an individual, he no longer pursues it for pleasure—he does so to keep from suffering.

When I would go to a theatre, and the curtain would be lowered for intermission, I would make a bee-line for the foyer. By the time I reached there I would have a cigarette between my lips and my lighter poised. I was not rushing to take that smoke in anticipation of the pleasure it would give me. I was hastening because I had been suffering for a smoke.

I would not leave one room for another without first feeling in my pockets to make certain I had my cigarettes. Many times, after preparing for bed, I would discover that my cigarettes were about gone. Rather than wake up in the night and not be able to satisfy my urge for a smoke, I would dress and drive down town to replenish my supply.

Filled ash-trays which give off a not too pleasant odor, burned holes in clothing and the alarming number of fires caused by smoking in bed . . . all added up to create a disgust for the habit.

I would secretly admire the man who, when offered a cigarette, would reply: "No thanks, I do not smoke."

"Must I be a slave to an insignificant thing like a cigarette?" I asked myself. I made another promise. I promised myself I would stop smoking.

A plan was worked out which proved so successful for me, I gave it to my radio and television audiences and have learned of thousands of people who have freed themselves from the habit. You may like to try it.

I decided that for a week I would not take my first smoke of the day until after breakfast. This promise was easy to keep because if I wanted a smoke I would merely tell myself: "It will be only a half-hour or so until I can gratify my wish."

During the second week, I would not take my first smoke until after lunch. This was not difficult either, because, as the urge to smoke would come, I could figure right to the minute when I would have my cigarette.

The next week I would take my first smoke after dinner. By this time the system was becoming accustomed to less and less of the tars and products of combustion, so this step did not prove difficult at all.

After this routine, I would go for a full day—24 hours—without a smoke; then 48 hours, three days, four days and on, up to a full week. After that I decided I would miss full weeks—two weeks—three weeks, and so on, until the urge to smoke had vanished.

I went as far as three weeks without a smoke and, when I tried one then, it tasted so vile I wanted nothing further to do with them.

How About Gambling?

Gambling can be controlled through reason, too. Money won through gambling never does one any good. It is always paid back with large interest.

One is often tempted to gamble because he hears of the large sums won by friends of his. They never tell of their losses, because if they did, they would show that over a period of time their losses greatly exceed their winnings.

Use your reasoning. Think of a single person who is living in the lap of luxury on an income gained exclusively from gambling. You may not think of one. On the other hand think of the hundreds of cases you hear about people who are merely existing on the barest necessities, because most of their income goes for gambling.

The only real satisfaction in life comes from achieving. When reflecting over your estate, how heart-warming it is to be able to say: "I created this fortune."

•　　•　　•　　•　　•

The pause at this station has enriched your life in many, many ways. You are gaining self-mastery. You will master habits instead of permitting them to master you. You have promised yourself to be truthful to yourself. In the future, before promising yourself anything, you will first make certain that it is a promise you can keep—then keep it.

Do not wait until you complete this journey before putting these principles to work. Start right now.

Make a resolution that, from this moment onward, you will be truthful with yourself and, so that you will begin to gain a new respect for yourself, make a promise, one that you can—and will—keep.

Here's a good promise for a start: decide that every chance you get, you will pay a compliment to the one with whom you come in contact. You will be amazed to find how friendly this world has become. We will learn more about the value of compliments at the next station on this journey, but now is a good time to form this new—and highly beneficial—habit.

GROWING RICH GRACEFULLY

Our fabulous journey is again coming to a brief halt, that we may learn another of life's great lessons.

You have the key to riches. They are yours to command. But, master your riches. Never let them master you.

At the age of thirty, Benjamin Franklin, in commenting on riches, made the wise remark: "Wealth is not his who has it, but his who enjoys it."

Wealth can become your master—or your servant. The time to learn how to enjoy your riches is when they are in the making. To wait until they have been accumulated is too late. By that time, habit patterns have been formed which will prevent one from enjoying that which he has.

A man of my acquaintance started life as a poor boy and determined to build a fortune for himself. He succeeded. Through hard work—and great sacrifice, by the time he had reached the age of 60, this man had accumulated enough money to last him throughout his life. Up to that time, however, he had never done anything to give him any enjoyment from his money. He lived in a small, inexpensive house, and his wife did all of the housework. This man would give more thought in spending a dollar than the man who had no more than a dollar to spend.

The big depression of 1929 came and wiped him out completely. This man spent the best years of his life accumulating money which vanished without having brought him a moment's enjoyment.

In San Francisco lives a man who owns most of a block of business houses. His income from rentals would permit him to live in one of the finest homes, and with a retinue of servants to care for his every need. But, how does he live? Money has become so much his god, he will not spend a penny unless it is absolutely necessary. He is a widower and lives alone in a small room, cooks his own meals and wears a suit of clothes until it almost falls apart. Very few common laborers would be content to live as he does. What can he get out of life?

Happiness Comes from Giving Happiness

The only real happiness is that which comes from making others happy. Our possessions, if used only for ourselves, will soon become commonplace and lack glamor. When we use our possessions to make others happy, they provide a never ending source of gratification.

Some years ago I spent a few weeks with a well known New England industrialist. His whole life was dedicated to bringing happiness into the lives of others. He had financed the building of an industrial school for boys. He had a large summer camp where children of the poor could spend their vacations under the care of experienced guides and nutritionist. Frequently he would anonymously help deserving couples.

"I retire at night with a smile on my face and a song in my heart," related this philanthropist as he explained the joy he was gaining through his gifts.

Growing rich gracefully really means to start building your estate with the right pattern in mind.

A building is planned in its entirety before a shovel is placed in the ground. You are about to begin laying the foundation for your estate of tomorrow. It should support a well conceived structure.

At a previous station on this journey, you made plans for a new standard of living. The plans were based on the type of possessions you should bring into being. At this station we are learning how to get the utmost from our possessions and, particularly, how to live with ourselves.

Some years ago, in one of my books, I coined an expression: The Fundamental Law of Giving. I pointed out that all receiving is preceded by giving—and that if one is not receiving enough —it is because he is not giving enough.

I learned this law of giving from Nature itself. Nowhere in Nature are there any signs of receiving; everything is giving. Do you know of any trees which fail to give up their leaves in the fall for fear they will not get new ones in the spring? In Nature, everything is giving. Yet human beings—products of Nature— try to live in direct violation of this fundamental law.

Not all giving is good. One can often do more harm through giving than by refusing to give.

In my younger days, I once found myself greatly in need of $500. There was a friend of mine who could easily afford to lend the money without making the slightest sacrifice. Due to our friendship, I felt certain I could get the money, so, at the first opportunity, I asked for it. To my great astonishment, this friend said:

"Ben, I could well afford to lend you the money, but I'm not going to do so," he responded grimly. "Lending money is one of the best ways to break friendships," he added.

I needed this money, so, not being able to borrow it, I worked out ways and means of earning it.

After my need for the money ceased, I thanked this friend of mine because of his refusal to lend me the sum asked for. Had he loaned me the money, the relief would merely have been temporary. While satisfying one need, I would be acquiring another obligation, which later must be met. As it was, I not only solved the existing problem, but had grown to the extent that it would be easy for me to care for similar future problems.

The best way to help a person is to help him to help himself. A gift of money might be of help momentarily—but if you help him to help himself—you have made a gift which will be everlasting.

In writing this book, I am giving no thought at all to the royalties I might earn. I am thinking of you. The letters which will come to me from people whose lives have been changed as a result of the book will be my greatest reward. I will gain a type of happiness I could never find in anything I might buy with royalties.

On my property there is a small grove of picturesque oak trees. I am planning on placing a number of large tables with benches under the trees. This being done it will be fun to invite groups of friends for outdoor picnics. The gaiety and laughter will pay me—a hundred times over—for the slight expense involved.

In Chicago lives a man who is gaining much happiness in life. He had an outdoor dining room added to his home; one which will accommodate groups of 200 people. This room is open in summer and can be closed and heated in winter. Every Sunday morning a delightful breakfast is served to a capacity group. Anyone can attend by writing for an invitation. An inspiring talk by some good speaker is always given during the breakfast.

"The friendships I have made through this Sunday get-together has greatly enriched my life," said this unusual man. You see, he is gaining happiness by making others happy.

Puget Sound, in the State of Washington, as you might know, is dotted with small islands; many of which are privately owned. The owner of one of these islands finds much happiness in an interesting way. He will sit on his veranda and, with a pair of powerful binoculars, scan the expanse of water before him. When he spots a couple in an inexpensive boat, he will signal to them to come to his island. When they arrive, he makes them most welcome. If it is mealtime, he invites them to have lunch or dinner with him. If it is between meals, he will serve refreshments of some kind.

I learned of this man through personal experience. One summer I was in one of the boats which he signalled.

"I look forward to my days on the island," this man exclaimed thoughtfully. "The real joy in owning this island is being able to share it with others."

While a guest in his home, he showed me an entire file filled with letters of appreciation from those he had entertained.

One capitalist told me of a unique plan he has. When asked

for a loan (and this is frequent) if he sees any merit in the appeal, he will make the prospective borrower a proposition.

"You acquire half of the amount through your own resources, without borrowing it and, I will lend you the other half," he tells the one seeking help.

"I seldom lend the money," he told me, with a twinkle in his eyes. "Either the borrower lacked courage to earn the first half, or, if he did, after reaching the half-way mark, he did not need a loan from me, because he could carry on until he secured all the funds he needed."

Growing Rich Gracefully

You have already decided upon your objective. You now know the path you will take to enable you to attain the standard of living you have set for yourself.

For your future peace of mind and happiness, see to it that as you go on through life, you will not only build a solid estate, but that you will gain the respect and admiration from all of those with whom you come in contact.

The owner of a chain of fine restaurants spends as much time as possible in his eating houses, so that he can personally meet those who patronize him. From a purely selfish standpoint, he gains materially by doing this because his customers appreciate the democratic way in which he does business. But, I am sure there is a bigger reason behind this man's actions. He loves people.

A good character is actually more of an asset than the money you have on deposit. With a good character, you seldom have any difficulty in financing any project in which you may become interested.

Financiers always make far more money on the use of other people's money than they do on their own. In fact, in their ventures, they use as little of their own money as they can.

An acquaintance of mine saw a chance to buy two lots in a rapidly growing neighborhood for $7,000, paying down only $1,000. It was only a short time before he sold them for $12,000.

This man did not make $5,000 on an investment of $7,000. He made $5,000 on an investment of only $1,000.

In Westchester County, New York, a man built a million dollar apartment house and started out with nothing at all. How did he do it? Quite simple. He went to the owner of a well located piece of property and made an interesting deal with him.

"I'll incorporate a company for the purpose of building a million dollar apartment house. You put up your lot for a proportionate amount of stock," he told this owner. Having a good character as well as a good idea, the deal was consummated.

If a lot has sufficient value, there are finance companies willing and anxious enough to supply necessary money for the building, accepting a mortgage on the building and lot as security.

The money was obtained for the apartment house. The former lot owner fared exceptionally well. The building was quickly filled with tenants and was later sold at a substantial profit.

After putting over similar deals, this imaginative man has retired with a fortune which started from nothing except a large amount of self-confidence.

• • • • •

As I think of one growing rich gracefully—I think of calmness. I picture the man who carries on day after day with efficiency, yet with that air of calmness that indicates he knows what he wants to do; he knows how to do it,—and, most important of all—is doing it.

He never appears ruffled, excitable or over-anxious. He moves constantly onward and upward with an air of contentment and great satisfaction. He takes time for recreation, not only because he is entitled to it, but because it is a definite part of his program of progress. And he enjoys his periods of recreation because his mind is at ease.

We are soon to reach our first plateau which will end this particular journey. Enroute you have acquired everything you need to assure a happy, successful life.

This journey has been an unusual one from the moment we decided upon taking it right up to the present. Here is a phase of the trip which will be surprising.

On all ordinary trips, after reaching the point of destination, one returns to his point of departure.

There is no return on this journey—because who among you would like to go back to the *you* as you were before embarking? No, we will remain on the first plateau for a proper period then carry on, seeking new trails to blaze.

Are You Too Old?

Before proceeding to our next station, there is one point I must discuss. I can almost hear some of you saying: "I agree with everything I have learned so far on this journey, but I'm too old to make a new start in life." To this I will reply: *"Nonsense!"*

There is only one time when you are too old to make a fresh start, and that is when you think you're too old—whether your chronological age is 50 or 80.

Delve into history and you'll learn of countless men and women who made their greatest contributions to mankind after they had passed so-called middle life.

A good formula to follow is to *live as though your life would go on forever.*

Naturally your life will not go on forever, but if you can live as though it would, many advantages would accrue in your favor.

You would *live longer.* The fear of death hastens death. After we pass the 50's we accept the thought we are growing old and we *act* old. We begin translating every ache or pain into terms of old age. Instead of looking for the cause of the ache or pain—and correcting the cause—we do nothing, taking it for granted that "at my age such things are expected."

If one is to live as though his life would go on forever, he would not hesitate entering new ventures, regardless of his existing age.

Human beings mature physically at varying ages, usually

between 16 and 20 years; yet, except in rare cases they are not mentally mature much before the age of 50. But, when we do reach the age of 50, too many of us begin preparing for death. This statement may seem a bit startling at first but, as you think about it you'll find it to be true.

As I say these things, I am speaking in generalities, of course. There are exceptions which prove the rule. When we think of people who have passed the age of 50, we refer to them as being old, or at least rather well along in years. When we, ourselves, pass 50, we begin thinking of ourselves as being old.

We hesitate taking up anything new, especially if it may require 5, 10, or 15 years to complete. Feeling that we are too old to make such an attempt.

At the close of spring each year, salesmen—and even merchants—will begin to prepare for a summer of poor business—and they are never disappointed. They do have a poor summer and why shouldn't they? They prepared for it.

So, too, with human beings regarding age. At the age of 50 they begin to let down, with the thoughts of the rapidly approaching 60's and 70's in mind.

Then we are subjected to the well-meaning suggestions of friends. We are urged not to do this and not to do that because "we are not as young as we used to be." In other words, everything possible is done by ourselves and others to give us an age consciousness. What a pity!

We have to reach an age of 50 before we really reach a stage of full mental maturity.

Our first 20 years are spent in growing out of childhood and gaining our primary education. Between 20 and 30 we begin "trying our wings" in getting an idea as to what life is all about. From 30 to 40, if we are fortunate, we become more or less settled in the work we intend to follow. The years from 40 to 50 are spent in gaining experience. Then what?

We awake to the realization we are old. We have spent 50 years in preparation. Preparation for what?

Does this seem to be the life Nature intended for us? I think not. Let us look into Nature a bit and think about the span of life allotted to forms of life other than human beings.

A dog, for example, reaches maturity at the age of 1 year; he lives an average of 10 years—or 10 times the period between birth and maturity. The average age of living creatures except human beings, is at least 7 times the period of elapsed time between birth and maturity.

Is Nature inconsistent? Did she intend a certain life span for all common forms of life—and for human beings, the highest form of all life—a life span of less than half that of the shortest lived creature? Certainly not! It would not be hard to prove that the normal life span of man is at least 125 years, and that, if we live and think as Nature intended we should, we, too, can reach this rightful age.

•   •   •   •   •

To those of you who have passed the age of 50, live according to every thought contained in this book just as religiously as though it were written especially for you. You'll almost feel a load falling from your shoulders as you take on a new lease of life.

Today we hear much about *psychosomatic* ailments; those physical conditions which emanate from the mind.

Do you know that aging is partly psychosomatic? We get old because we expect to get old. We have so thoroughly accepted the three score years and ten theory that, after we pass 50, we feel we are rapidly approaching the end. We withdraw from activities which carry over into the future and begin living in the past. We are playing right in the hands of father time in hastening the processes of aging.

Think of yourself as you were, let us say, 15 or 20 years younger than you are now.

Begin applying every principle given so far. You will be surprised the next time you step to your mirror. Your reflection will show a more youthful expression to your face. There will be a gleam in your eye which has been missing for many years. Your friends will wonder what process of rejuvenation you have resorted to.

Do you know, that in the realm of accomplishment, a man of

full maturity has an advantage over the younger man? Through his greater number of years he has had the opportunity to accumulate more knowledge. His judgement and decisions are based upon ripened thinking.

Think of the ages of most of the presidents of the United States, and the judges in the Supreme Court of the United States. Many of the greatest world leaders are well past 60.

So, if you have felt that you might be too old to benefit by this fabulous journey we have been taking—shame on you.

● ● ● ● ●

I was once a guest speaker at the Detroit Yacht Club. I took as my subject: 125—Your Normal Life Span. After the meeting was over, a man approached me and remarked: "Ben, in my younger days I always yearned to take up the study of microscopy, but at that time I couldn't afford to buy a good microscope. Now, since I can afford one, I thought I was too old for such a pastime. But since hearing you talk, I decided I'll go out and buy the best instrument on the market."

I happened to meet that man several years later. He actually looked younger than he had when I first met him. The reason? It's simple. Instead of living in the past as an old man he is keeping his mind active on constructive things.

No! You are never too old to gain full benefit from this journey to the land of better living.

Station 12

YOUR FIRST PLATEAU

When I arrived in Hawaii on my first visit to our 50th state, all passengers were up bright and early and crowded on the observation deck waiting for their first glimpse of the glamorous islands. Nature took part in the welcome by placing a background of fleecy clouds in back of old Diamond Head so that, with the rays of the early morning sun, it was a breath-taking picture.

As I recall the excited faces of all on board, I think of readers with me now on this fabulous journey we are taking together and realize that the eagerness to capture the first glimpse of the "Promised Land" will be even more intense. In the former case, the people were absorbing something which would soon be a memory. On this journey, we are about to view a Shangri-la of our own making—the threshold of a new life of fulfillment.

Have we reached our final abode where we shall dwell from now on? No! We shall tarry here until we have become thoroughly accustomed to the many blessings and possessions we have acquired on this journey. Then we shall seek new trails to blaze.

• • • • •

Right now, we are ready for a great transition. Our self-made Shangri-la is one that is definitely real to our mental selves, and clearly visible to our mind's eye. Our physical eyes see the same environment we had before we started the journey—the same house, same wardrobe, same occupation, same financial situation.

But, our attitude toward all of our material possessions of the past has changed completely. Any feeling of lack, discouragement or self-pity we might have had, has vanished completely. We have a sense of joy we have never had before because we now have a clear vision of the life we want—the life we know will be ours.

As we started this journey, we learned that mind is man and our bodies are merely utilities. Our minds have taken this crowning journey; our physical beings have remained to "keep the home fires burning" until the glorious moment of reunion.

Permit me to tell you a story which was published many, many years ago. Although strictly fiction, there is a principle involved in the story which is definitely sound.

There are two principle characters: a man of great wealth who was in very poor health, and a poor man with glowing health. These two men envied each other. The rich man would gladly surrender his wealth for a healthy body. The poor man would quickly give up his health for material riches.

According to the tale, a world famed surgeon discovered a way to exchange brains from one body to another. This rich man made a deal with the poor man to exchange their brains. The rich man would then be poor, but with a fine, healthy body. The poor man would be rich, but with a body of aches and pains.

The operation was successful. The poor man became rich, the rich man became poor. But, let us see what happened.

The former rich man had always had a consciousness of success. He could never think of himself in any other way except as a success. So, with such a concept, he had soon accumulated another fortune. But, along with his success consciousness, he had always been concerned with his body. He was always fearing physical ailments and each time he would have a slight pain or an ache he would enlarge upon it. So, with this type of a concept, his radiant body soon became weak and infirm. In other words, he returned to his former condition—a rich man with an ailing body.

Now let us see what happened with the newly made rich man:
This man always had had a poor consciousness. He could

never think of himself as being anything else except poor. With his acquired wealth he had not established a new standard of balanced living, but went on making one foolish investment after another. The old adage: "A fool and his money are soon parted," proved to be true in his case. His money soon disappeared, and he was, once again, a poor man. But, how about his body? That's a different story. He had never given any thought to his body, so far as illness is concerned. He always thought of himself as being in good health. So, without "nursing" the ailments he inherited when he traded brains they faded away and in time his body was, like his former one, in very good health.

The story ends with both of the principals back where they were in the beginning.

Now then—what is the lesson we shall learn from this story? I will refer to a statement made many stations back: "You Are What You Think You Are!"

You Are What You Think You Are!

You were as you were due to the thoughts you had held regarding yourself.

On this journey you have gained an entirely new concept of yourself. You now know beyond all contradiction that the future will be of your own making and that you will make it as you want it to be.

You have gained a consciousness of success which knows no failure. You have learned the satisfaction of achievement and will gain your greatest happiness as you see your plans take shape and your objectives become realities.

An experience of mine will fit in exceptionally well at this point.

Salesmanship has always been a pet of mine. I love to sell. I love to teach others to sell.

Some years ago in New York City, I was engaged to give a 30-minute talk to a sales group every Monday morning, the object being to help the men start the week properly inspired.

There were about 30 men whom I would talk to on these occasions. I am quite sure I was helping them. Their sales were good and the men seemed happy with what I gave to them each week. There was, however, one condition regarding these men which puzzled me. Some of the most highly educated men on the sales staff were low in their sales; some of the men with less education were up on top.

Common sense told me that having a good education was no barrier, but why the difference? I decided to find out.

I began making a psychological study of a salesman; I wanted to discover just what made him tick.

A discovery was made which, since then, has helped thousands of salesmen to improve their records.

I discovered that, although a thorough knowledge of one's work is essential, it is second in importance to the impression one has of *himself*. The big salesman is big because he *sees* himself as a big salesman. The mediocre salesman is as he is because he *sees* himself as just doing well enough to get by.

One Monday morning, I explained to my men that I wanted them to join with me in an experiment.

I asked them to start the day by repeating to themselves— several times—"I Am a Great Salesman!" During the day, while going from one prospect to another, instead of holding negative thoughts, such as: "I wonder if he will grant me an interview." "I wonder if he'll turn me down like the last one did," etc., etc., to continue with the declaration: "I Am a Great Salesman." At night before retiring, again repeat several times: "I Am a Great Salesman!"

"That seems inconsistent," interrupted one of the salesmen. "I know I'm not a good salesman and for me to tell myself I am a great salesman, is just kidding myself," he continued.

"Why *are* you *not* a good salesman?" I laughed sympathetically.

His face reddened as he realized that he was a poor salesman because he had been *seeing* himself as a poor salesman.

In the room where the sales meetings were held was a totem pole reaching to the ceiling. On this pole was a row of small hooks from the floor to the top. Each man had a card bearing his name, in the corner of which was an eyelet so that the card could be hung on one of the hooks. As a salesman would climb in sales, his card would be hung on a hook higher up.

The card of the salesman who first took issue with me regarding my theory started to climb. It went up from hook to hook until it nearly reached the top.

"To what do you attribute your meteoric rise?" I asked this man at the next sales meeting.

With a slight touch of crimson on his cheeks, he replied: "I Am a Great Salesman!" And, his sales were proving it to be true.

This man was just getting by so long as he saw himself as a poor salesman. The moment he changed his mental picture of himself, he began to go places.

There was general improvement among nearly all of the men. One man, however, whose card occupied a middle position before the experiment, remained in the same position afterwards. I wondered why. Later I learned that he had been telling his associates that my theory was "just the bunk."

This Principle *Not* Black Magic

To those who understand the mind and how it operates, the reason why this principle is so sound is perfectly obvious. The subconscious mind follows the pattern established by the conscious mind.

If a salesman holds a picture of himself as being a poor salesman, the subconscious mind will direct him in thought and action—to *make* him a poor salesman. His presentation will be halting and faulty. He will lack the forcefulness to properly impress his prospect.

If he sees himself as a great salesman, he is guided in the thoughts he will express. An enthusiasm will be built up which will reflect in his voice and manner—and which will impress the prospect.

This principle is not only effective in the profession of salesmanship, but in every department of life.

In my earlier days I operated a modest sized advertising agency in New York. We specialized in direct-by-mail-advertising, which meant that many sales letters were used.

Not feeling that I was capable of writing good sales letters, I engaged outside talent to write them.

"Why can't *I* write good sales letters?" I asked myself on an occasion when I had turned down several which had been written for me, and which I could not accept as good. As I thought about it, I realized that I could not write good letters because *I thought I could not write good letters.*

I changed my mental picture of myself. I sold myself on the idea that I *could* write good sales letters. The letters I wrote for clients pulled such good results, I soon found myself well occupied writing letters—and at an exceptionally good fee. I was a poor sales letter writer so long as I saw myself as such. I became a good sales letter writer the moment I began seeing myself as one.

The best parents are those who *see* themselves as being good parents. They are guided by the great intelligence of the subconscious mind in doing the right things to make them good parents.

It Can't Be Done, But Here It Is

The late Charles F. Kettering who, for years, successfully headed the research division of General Motors, once said: "In hiring men for my research laboratory, I try to select those who have not yet learned the things which cannot be done. From them I get some of my best inventions."

A very large percentage of our greatest inventions represent ideas which at one time were considered as being beyond reason. The popular impression that "they couldn't be done" held back possible development until someone came along, not knowing they couldn't be done.

A man was leaving the employ of one company to accept an offer with another; an offer for a far better job at a much larger salary.

"You'll never make good in that job," warned the first employer as he tried to convince his man to stay.

For the first few months the man did not make good, and it looked like he would soon be looking for a new job.

One day he asked himself: "What's the matter with me? Why am I making a failure of this job?"

As he reflected over his past, it dawned upon him that, almost daily, the warning: "You'll never make good in that job," kept ringing through his mind.

With resolute determination he began building on the thought: "I *will* make good—I *am* making good!" The tide turned. He not only made good, but before long he had been given a substantial increase in salary.

"You fooled me," said his employer as he told him of the raise. "For the first few months you were here I was afraid I would have to let you go. Suddenly your work started showing improvement, until today, you are one of my best men." You see? This man had accepted a negative suggestion and was acting upon it. The moment he began *seeing* himself as making good, he started to climb.

I Can—I Will—I Am

You have learned that you CAN accomplish great things. You have resolved that you WILL accomplish great things. My work, however, would not be complete if I did not impress upon you a great truth.

The word "Will" has an indefinite aspect. You might decide that you will do a certain thing, but the time for action is not fixed. It could be tomorrow, or next week, next month, or next year. Or, it could even be several years from now. And, if you should do it eventually, you would be keeping your promise.

We meet so many people who are *going* to do this—and *going* to do that, but they never reach the time for action.

You, now that you have reached this first plateau, must back your intentions with *action*. You will change the *you* who existed before this revealing journey into the *you* who will correspond with the new picture you now hold of yourself.

An acquaintance of mine told me a bit about his life and how he had held himself back through procrastination; by always *going* to do a certain thing, instead of *doing* it.

He told me that there was a certain enterprise in which he was sure he could make good. He decided he would go into it—but he did not back his plans with action. In the fall he was *going* to start in the spring. In the spring he felt that, with summer coming on, it would be better to start in the fall, and on and on it went; one postponement after another.

Finally he became disgusted with allowing himself to delay action from season to season, so he made the start. He made good—and in a very big way.

"Think of the years of success and greater happiness I lost," he admitted remorsefully.

Overcoming Procrastination

Do you know why most people procrastinate—and how to overcome procrastination? It is extremely simple.

The same principle which will convert an ordinary salesman into a great salesman will work like magic in aiding one to overcome procrastination.

Begin creating a mental pattern of yourself as one who does things *now*. Know that after you have an objective and your reasoning faculties tell you it is one that you *can* attain, the impulse will come to make a start at the earliest opportunity. See yourself as one who likes action. You will reach a point where you will not waste a moment in starting anything which will result in your ultimate good.

You are now on your first plateau where you will make realities of the objective you decided upon during your journey.

It might be a splendid idea if we take a moment or two in reliving parts of our journey so that we will not miss any of the golden opportunities we found en route.

Station #1. *Happiness.* You learned that through living happy, you will not only gain more from life, but that happiness is really essential for success.

In talking about happiness, I am not trying to create the impression that one should wear a continual grin like Alice in Wonderland's Cheshire cat. The type of happiness I refer to is that warm glow around your heart which makes you feel that God is in his heaven and all is well on earth. You are contented with the thoughts you are thinking and the things you are doing. You should be—and I am sure you are—happy right now.

Station #2. *Enthusiasm.* Enthusiasm is a motivating force

which makes action toward an objective a decided pleasure: even fun.

At this station you were not only advised to develop enthusiasm, but were shown how to do so. It might be well for you to review the notes you made at the station to make certain you will not be missing the added zest enthusiasm will add to your plans.

I can sense your enthusiasm right now. You have so many wonderful things to look forward to, your eyes are like those of a child as he gets his first peep at the Christmas tree and toys on Christmas morning.

Station #3. *Happy Discontent.* Tell the average person that he must first become discontented with his lot as is before he will begin to improve himself, and he will look at you in wonderment. But this is not true with you.

No longer will you be contented with anything but the best. You know that success, happiness and abundance is your rightful heritage and you know how to get what you want.

Henry Ford said that he kept his eye on the young man who showed signs of being dissatisfied, especially if he thought he had anything to offer in the way of improving things. "The restless boy," he said, "the one who wants to know *why* things are as they are, and why they can't be done better, is the one who shows signs of possible leadership."

Station #4. *Action!* One might move forward through sheer will power, but his task will be hard and often discouraging. At this station of the journey, the traveller was spurred on through a combination of happiness and enthusiasm; and because he knows where he is going—and how to get there.

Had there ever been any tendencies toward procrastination in your make-up, they are gone. You are now guided by a combination of three watch-words: Objective—Plan—Action.

Station #5. *Continuity.* Continuity of action was the lesson learned at this station. No day should pass without seeing progress. On this journey the traveller learned that, although he may pause occasionally to enjoy his progress and for earned relaxation and recreation, his general direction should be continually onward and upward.

Station #6. *Components.* An architect, in designing a building, decides in advance every item which enters into its construction. You have already determined what, to you, constitutes success. You learned while pausing at this station that it is advisable to tabulate the elements necessary to bring into fruition success as you want it.

Station #7. *Analysis—Synthesis.* A building is built brick by brick; a journey is covered mile by mile; a painting is completed stroke by stroke. Dwelling mentally on a completed whole often makes the task of achievement appear laborious. Here you learned to focus attention on the individual steps; each one— through this process—appears simple—and *is* simple.

Learning this added materially to your enthusiasm—which, in turn brought on a greater sense of happiness.

Station #8. *Major—Minor.* The key to simplicity in accomplishment was obtained at this station. While acquiring the type of satisfaction you desire is your major objective, each step toward the attainment of that objective should be considered as a minor objective.

As you tackle each minor objective—with a feeling it is a major objective—you will find yourself climbing over minor objective after minor objective—until you reach your major objective.

Form a habit of thinking of minor objectives in connection with any desire you may have. It will help you materially in getting yourself into action—thus preventing old man procrastination from scoring a victory.

Station #9. *Your New Standard of Living.* You live through a daily succession of habits from the moment you arise in the morning until you retire at night.

Now that you have the key which will open the door to abundance, you should plan to rise to a higher standard of living. This does not mean the development of a boastful, show-off attitude; but a standard of living in keeping with your new capabilities to achieve.

Station #10. *A New Life Pattern.* We all exist, but very few actually live. Our todays are merely periods of time which followed our yesterdays. This, however, is no longer true with you. You have created a new life pattern; one replete with success, vibrant health—and happiness.

Remember what you have already learned about habit and its power. By now you should be well on your way toward the creation of new habits—a new life pattern.

Station #11. *Growing Rich Gracefully*. There is nothing more repellent than one who continually exhibits his newly acquired wealth. It is an art to have wealth and not become obnoxious in the presence of those less fortunate.

As you acquire your individualized form of success, you now know ways and means of causing your good fortune to endear yourself to others.

NEW TRAILS TO BLAZE

It hasn't been long since you began mapping the journey you have just completed. You have been a good traveller.

As you enjoy the results of your present achievement, you will begin thinking of new trails to blaze. Your first objective might have been riches; you may now like to enter the cultural stratas of life, or become proficient in some of the arts, crafts or sciences. You have acquired the habit of travelling ever onward and upward.

(Although it is true that it has been only a matter of a very short time since you started this journey, and that it would be physically impossible for you to attain your objectives—or even part of them—in such a short time, I am continuing just as though your objectives are *now realities; because they will be realities*. It will not be long before I will be leaving this work to begin blazing new trails of my own, but before doing so I wish to give you a road map to guide you throughout your life.)

When you first began mapping your journey; when you started thinking in terms of the material things which you felt would make you happy, it seemed as though you had encompassed everything. I can actually imagine how you would say to yourself: "Boy! If I get all of those things, my life will be complete."

Permit me to repeat a statement I have made before: "Nothing stands still—it either moves forward or backward."

Were you to stop after having acquired your objectives, life would soon lose its lustre. You would take everything you have for granted, and your zest for life would diminish.

I have frequently been a guest at a club which has a membership made up largely of men who "have arrived" from a finan-

157

cial point of view. Studying the faces of those in the reading room—to the thinking man—provides an object lesson. The look of animation, of eagerness, characteristic of them in their days of climbing, has vanished. When their watches tell them it is time to leave for home, you sense the "ho-hum" attitude as they signal their chauffeurs to take them home. The attitude of those affluent men is no different than that of the man who has labored all day at some menial work and who, at the close of the day with a "ho-hum" feeling departs for his humble abode.

This will *not* be true with you. After you attain the objectives which will give you future security—and put you on the standard of living you have decreed for yourself, you are going to blaze new trails, so that the spirit of adventure and accomplishment will be forever vibrant in your heart.

One day the president of a large chain of stores invited me to lunch; he wanted my counsel.

"Why is it I am not happy?" he asked. "I am a millionaire. My home life is happy. There are no particular business problems disturbing me."

This man had built a tremendous business and, due to the efficient men placed in charge of various departments, it was running smoothly. He had a pretentious home which with sufficient help, was also running smoothly.

Most men in this position would feel they were in heaven, but this man was unhappy. Why? He had not created new interests.

"All that glitters is not gold," said the Prince of Morocco in *The Merchant of Venice*. We might paraphrase that thought with another one. "All who are envied are not necessarily happy."

A worried woman once told me that her husband, although extremely successful from a financial point of view, had often expressed the wish that he was dead. She invited me to visit them at their home to see if I could find a reason for his mental depression.

It didn't take long to learn *why* he was depressed. He had reached the top in his business. There was little he needed of a material nature. His future was secure.

But there was nothing to excite his interest; to cause him to look forward to the tomorrows, instead of living in the "good old times" of his yesterdays.

I started fishing around to see if I could discover any latent interest. I was not successful at first. I would bring up subject after subject without striking a spark. Accidentally I struck pay dirt when I inquired about a ship model on the mantel. It was a miniature of the *Santa Maria,* the flagship used by Columbus on his historic expedition.

"I made that 30 years ago," he said as a gleam of pride shone in his eyes.

"That's a marvelous pastime," I exclaimed as my eyes surveyed every detail of the ship.

"Why don't you continue with your hobby and build the two caravels which completed Columbus' initial fleet, the *Pinta* and the *Nina?*" I added.

"Wel-l-l, I don't know," he drawled as his eyes stared into space for an answer. Then turning to me, with an almost look of victory, he declared with growing exuberance: "I think I'll do it."

A corner of his garage was fitted out with a work bench and a complete assortment of tools, and model boat building began. I learned that he did make models of the other two boats of Columbus, and is now happily working on a model of the most famous ship in the annals of the American Navy: the *Constitution,* familiarly known as *"Old Ironsides."*

"He is not the same man," his wife said happily. "The hours he spends with his hobby enable him to overcome the tension accumulated during the days in his office. I haven't seen him as happy in years."

• • • • •

Do you enjoy music? "Yes," you might say, "but I would never take it up at my age."

A piano teacher once told me that the best student she had was a man who didn't start in until he was 73 years old. If you like music, Nature is telling you that you can learn to play an instrument.

A young person might have to be urged to practice on a musical instrument, because his mind is on so many other things he would rather be doing. When an adult takes up music because he *wants* to be able to play an instrument, practice becomes fun.

The chief of police of a western city, a man quite well along in years, took up playing the organ as a pastime.

"I never expect to be a great organist," he told me, "but it does relax me and gives me a diversion from my regular daily duties."

All of the men under this chief know about his hobby which indicates he enjoys talking about it. There is no danger that this man will ever reach a stalemate in his occupation. He keeps his interest alive and lives in the future as well as the past.

Would you like to write? Most people wish they could write, so it is quite likely you will answer this question in the affirmative. You will admit you would like to write, but you have no idea you ever could write.

A woman who admitted she would like to write said she could give three reasons why she would never be able to do so. 1) She did not have enough mastery of the English language. 2) She would not know how to begin writing a story, and 3) No one would buy the story if she did write one.

Of course you know that these were not reasons—they were merely excuses.

One—at any age—can readily improve his English. There are many ways. You will find home study courses which will assist you in improving your use of the English language. Keep a dictionary by your side as you read. Any time you encounter a word not familiar to you—look it up. If you learn but one new word each day, that will add 365 words to your vocabulary in a year.

Here, too, you will find many ways to learn the technique of story writing. There are a few good home courses which teach various forms of writing: newspaper, magazine, books, etc.

As to this last excuse: "No one would buy the story if she should write one." Editors and publishers are always seeking good material. As she develops the consciousness that she can write, and backs it up with a sincere program which will give her the know-how, she *will* write material acceptable to editors and publishers.

A few years ago a woman wrote me a rather lengthy letter in which she outlined a problem she had. She expressed herself so beautifully—and put over her thought so well—I asked her why she had never considered writing as a career. She had never thought of it, she admitted.

If you drop a pebble into a pond, the ripples go, in enlarging circles, until they reach the outermost edge of the water.

Drop a thought into a receptive mind and it will go, in enlarging circles, until it reaches the outermost boundary of the consciousness.

The suggestion I gave to the lady regarding her manner of written expression proved to be a thought dropped into a receptive mind. It kept enlarging until she began to *see* herself as a writer. She started writing; had a few rejections, but kept on. Today her work is quite well known to the reading public.

•   •   •   •   •

Would painting interest you? If you would like to paint, it is more than likely that you can paint.

An important executive was compelled to remain at home because one of his children had contracted a communicable disease.

Loafing is one of the hardest things an active man can do, and this man was no exception. He had to find something to occupy his time.

It so happened that his young son had received a painting set consisting of a few tubes of colors and a brush or two. Although this man had never tried his hand at painting, he found it fascinating to take different colors and apply them to the canvas to form different shapes.

To his astonishment, he found he could paint a picture which, although not a masterpiece, was at least recognizable. His interest in painting grew and, after the quarantine was taken from his house, he purchased a complete outfit of paints, brushes, canvas, etc.

Painting became this man's spare time occupation and gave him a happy respite from the pressure of his daily business.

Painting is a creative diversion. Many of our greatest people, such as Winston Churchill and Dwight D. Eisenhower, find pleasurable relief from their days work through painting.

Why not try your hand? You might be happily surprised as you find your colors taking shape on the canvas.

•   •   •   •   •

One of the joys of travelling is one's ability to speak the language of the country in which he is visiting. It is also a pleasure to be able to converse with a foreigner in his own tongue. So, as a new trail to blaze, perhaps the study of a new language will provide you with a golden opportunity.

And, there is no law preventing you from learning more than one language in addition to your own. I have many friends who are capable of speaking four, five and six different languages.

In New York, a friend of mine took me to a Chinese restaurant for dinner. When the waiter came for our order, I was amazed to hear my friend give the order in Chinese.

Noting my surprise, this man told me that some day he wanted to visit China and he knew it would be more fun if he could make himself understood in Chinese.

A banker found an outlet by making pictures inlaid in wood. He has produced some of the most magnificent pictures in wood I have ever seen. Pieces of his work have been on exhibition in several of the largest cities in the country. This man told me that his work, as successful as he had been in it, was beginning to lose its lustre. His diversion not only gave him a new pleasure in life, but actually renewed interest in his banking activities.

The president of a large company producing well known dairy products found a new trail to blaze when he became interested in stone cutting and polishing. As he exhibits his handiwork, he takes pleasure in referring to himself as a lapidary.

A famous Hollywood actor keeps himself active between pictures in a well equipped laboratory he has created for himself. I have visited very few commercial laboratories as completely equipped as this one. As a result of his pastime, he has made valuable contributions to science.

Many men, after reaching the zenith of their success, will go in for such he-man activities as big game hunting or exploring.

We will find those who will take a single subject and go in for intensive research pertaining to the subject, learning all they can regarding it.

Find a Trail—Then Blaze It

Up to this point I have been throwing out mere suggestions. Like the clerk in a store who will show the prospective customer one necktie after another, hoping he will see just one he likes.

I might have aroused your interest long before this. On the other hand I may be miles from that which would fire your imagination. But, I am sure, you understand my motive. Once you reach the heights to which you aspired to climb, you will not want to remain there permanently. You will stay for a period sufficient to appraise—and enjoy—your accomplishments, but without new trails to blaze, you would soon weary of what you have.

"Anticipation is greater than realization," said a great philosopher. Some might ask: "Why strive for something if you'll not enjoy it after you get it?"

The answer to this is found in the first few lines of this book. Success is not a destination, but a journey!

On this journey you have thrilled over each turn in the road as new vistas of happiness and opportunity were unfolded before you. Achievement is the greatest satisfaction in life.

When a man goes deep sea fishing, does he find his greatest thrill after a large fish lies dead on the deck of his boat? If you're a fisherman, you know this is not so. It was when he was winning the fight with the monster and gradually pulling him in closer to his boat.

In big game hunting, the biggest thrill does not come when viewing a lifeless tiger at your feet. No! It was when you proved your superiority by outwitting him.

Do you recall the conversation I had with the wealthy department store executive regarding his success? I asked him when he felt he had gained his greatest thrill in life. He replied: "It was not when I *had* money; but when I first began to *make* money.

You will gain great success; of this I am sure. But do not consider a big income and a fine home as the end of the road. The moment you become accustomed to your new life pattern— your new standard of living—you will take your condition for granted—and, unless you have discovered new trails to blaze, your enthusiasm for life will wane.

Peace of Mind

The Alpha and Omega of all desire is peace of mind. Not everyone knows this. Or at least we do not think through far enough to realize the ultimate object of our desires.

The poor man wants riches, not merely for the luxuries the money will provide but, in back of the desire is a longing (often subconsciously) for security—peace of mind.

Peace of mind is a state of mind. It is not something we acquire, but something we express. It does not come from what we get, but how we use that which we have. It is that condition we reach when we are satisfied with the thoughts we are thinking and the things we are doing.

There is a distinction between satisfaction and peace of mind. We learned while stopping at Station #3 "Happy Discontent," we should not become contented with our status in life because contentment with what we have done with our lives thwarts progress.

Discontent has often been classed as the mother of invention. One with a constructive mind will, if discontented with anything, give serious thought to developing ways and means of improving it.

A thought provoking quotation from the works of Seneca is "Nothing is more dishonorable than an old man, heavy with years, who has no further evidence of having lived long, except his age."

What I am leading up to is this: Now that you are on the first plateau which represents the attainment of the objectives you laid out for yourself, do not become contented in the feeling that you have arrived, that this is it. Yes, you have arrived at the first plateau, but before you permit your present circumstances to become commonplace, you will move on to a higher plateau through starting on the new trails you will blaze.

As indicated by the several examples I have given, your objectives between you and your higher plateau need not be material. Objectives which will lift you mentally and spiritually will mean more to you at this phase of your life.

I asked one woman who was well on her way toward the first plateau—the attainment of her material objective—what she intended to do after all of her objectives were realities. She replied: "I want to spend as much time as I can in making people happy."

I know this woman means it, because now she is doing much in her limited time. And she has a unique way in giving happiness —a way which gives lasting happiness. Instead of giving temporary relief by handing out bits of money, she does all she can to help a person to help himself. If she finds a man making a small income because he is in the wrong job, she will help him to get the training which will put him into a better paying one. When she finds a woman who is eager to help her husband, but who lacks training to get a profitable job, she will often find ways of helping the wife to get the training.

Live in Harmony

See to it that one of your big objectives is to have harmony in the home.

A prominent industrialist, when engaging an employee for an important position, will investigate the home-life as well as the ability and integrity of the applicant. He has found that employees with inharmony in the home were never as efficient as those who lived in an atmosphere of harmony.

As to peace of mind, it is easy to understand that there will be none in homes of bickering, nagging and quarreling.

Happiness in the home does not just happen. You must plan for it. And the rewards are so worth while.

A man once told me he is glad to leave home in the morning

and dreads returning at night, due to marital inharmony. It is safe to assume there is no peace of mind in this home.

Another man told me he looked forward to returning to his home of love and harmony. You do not have to guess to know this one has peace of mind.

I will close this chapter with a beautiful quotation from the pen of Henry van Dyke:

"Peace of mind. To be glad of life because it gives you the chance to love and to work and to play and to look up at the stars, to be satisfied with your possessions but not contented with yourself until you have made the best of them, to despise nothing in the world except falsehood and meanness and to fear nothing except cowardice, to be governed by your admiration rather than by your disgusts, to covet nothing that is your neighbors except his kindness of heart and gentleness of manners, to think seldom of your enemies, often of your friends, and to spend as much time as you can, with body and with spirit, in God's out-of-doors, these are little guide-posts on the footpaths to peace."

RETROSPECTION
INSPECTION
ANTICIPATION

Retrospection

The true past departs not; no truth or goodness realized by man ever dies, or can die; but all is still here, and, recognized or not, lives and works through endless changes," said the English essayist, Thomas Carlyle.

The attitude one has towards the past, present and future plays an important part in his success and happiness.

Throughout these pages, we have been concerned with the past, present and future by changing thought patterns established in the past, so that our actions of the present will bring into fulfillment the type of future we desire.

I feel, however, it will be well if we round out this work, which we might refer to as *mental re-education,* by specifically considering the past, present and future, and their relationship with each other.

First we will consider the past; retrospection.

There are two distinct phases of the past: material and memory.

Every material possession you own is from the past; the house you live in, the clothes you wear, the car you drive, the food you have on your pantry shelves. Everything you see advertised for sale are products of the past. In fact, it is an impossibility to obtain anything from the present or future. Items now in the process of making will be products of the past when they reach you.

Memories of the past—to most people—are disconcerting. Memories of unpleasant experiences give rise to self-pity and memories of pleasant experiences cause one to linger on thoughts of the "good old days."

A man who had been extremely successful in the business world lost everything he had through a chain of unfortunate circumstances. He took a job as a salesman in order to meet his living expenses.

This man's mind was so fixed on his successes of the past, he would not be with a prospect more than a minute or two, before he would begin to reminisce about his past. Instead of telling the prospect about the product he was selling, he would take his time telling about the big business he once controlled. Naturally this man did not succeed as a salesman. In a few cases he would receive orders due to sympathy—but never through his ability to sell.

He came to me to cry on my shoulder, and with the hope I could give him a solution to his problem.

"You still have the ability you had when you first organized your business—plus several years of added experience," I told him. "Start planning on a new business and use salesmanship as a means of building up an income sufficient to enable you to do so," I added. I told him of the genuine fun he could have in rebuilding, and how much satisfaction he would have in proving that he might have been down—but he was not out.

The moment that man changed his attitude toward his past and present things began to happen. Today he has a bigger business than the one he had and which had been giving him an excuse for self-pity.

"I am happier than I ever have been," he said with satisfaction one day as we lunched at his club.

Here is a truth I want you to fix in your mind. *Every memory you have regarding the past is good.* You might take issue with this—for the moment; but, if you will *think* as you read further, you will be happy to agree with me.

Success comes from doing the things you know you ought to do, and in not doing the things you know you ought not to do.

Your memories of the past will guide you as to the things you should not repeat in the future, as well as those things you should repeat.

Be happy for every experience you have ever had; whether it appeared good or bad at the time you had it. It will help you materially in working out plans for the future.

"Everything is for the best," I often heard as a child. It meant little to me then, because I felt I had so many reasons to disprove it. Now, as I study the statement, I realize that it will be true, if you make it so.

You are as you are because of every experience you have had from the time of your birth to the present. Remove any of your past experiences and you would not be as you are.

A very simple illustration is a cake. A cake is as it is, due to all the ingredients entering into it. If any one of the ingredients had been left out, the cake would be different.

The journey which we just completed started in the past and ended in the past. It will prove to be the most important step you have ever taken. You have revised your viewpoint on life completely. You know beyond any shadow of a doubt that the future is of your own making and that you will make it as you want it. This journey—an experience of the past—has such a vitally important bearing on your future, it overshadows every former experience you have ever had. Every other experience sinks into insignificance in comparison. From this moment onward, appraise every thought you may have of the past as to its value in connection with your future.

Very few realize that all excuses for present failures stem from the past. One's past will appear as a large, dark closet filled with ghosts and hob-goblins. To him the past is a maze of bad luck and sad experiences. He fears peeping into the past because those things which have been haunting him may jump out at him.

With your new viewpoint regarding the past, instead of fearing it, you will delve down into it for the help you may gain in connection with your present problem. There will be no ghosts and hob-goblins in your closet because you will keep the light turned on, allowing everything to remain in full view.

Be glad you're alive. Be glad you are just as you are because you'll gain so much fun in changing yourself to fit into your new life pattern.

Do you recall the first station we visited on this journey—Happiness? Although happiness was discussed from the standpoint of what we were about to acquire, you can now understand that complete happiness—without accepting the entire past as being good—is not possible. So, it will be well to review the notes you made at that station and add them to what you have just received—and you'll have the formula for complete happiness.

If I should plot my life as an economist plots business trends, the ups and downs would make the line on the chart look like saw teeth. As I now compare my present with my past, it is easy to see where my failures contributed more to my present success than did my former successes.

This will be true with you once you learn to study your past purely for the lessons it contains. You will prove conclusively that the statement: "Everything is for the best," applies to you.

Inspection

We have surveyed the past now let us examine the present. What period of time constitutes the present? Far less than one might think. Let us see if we cannot draw a word picture of the present. Imagine two large reels of tape; the tape slowly unwinding from one reel to the other. Midway between the two reels is a sharp blade under which the tape passes. The tape is moving from right to left. Label the right reel "future" and the left reel "past." Here is the big surprise. The present is the fine edge of the sharp blade under which the tape is passing.

In other words, the present is just a timeless, imaginary dividing line between the past and future. I started this thought in the past; I will finish it in the future.

Since there is no time in the present, you will understand that the only time you have to do anything is right now. You can't start something yesterday, any more than you can start something tomorrow. You can decide that you *will* do something tomorrow, but you can't start it until tomorrow becomes today.

It has been said—and truthfully so—that one's problems from the past, coupled with fear of the future, is what makes the present so hard.

Do you know that better than 90 per cent of the hardships the average person endures are mental—not physical—and are unnecessary? Such a statement seems so unbelievable, an explanation is necessary.

The facts I am about to present resulted from a survey I made, in which I attempted to learn why people are as they are—and what might be done to change their circumstances.

Let us look into a few cases so that I can prove the statement I have just made.

A young man came to me in desperate circumstances. His rent was due and he was soon to be evicted. His credit had been cut off so far as daily provisions were concerned. His wife was expecting a baby within five months. He had no income.

I intentionally aroused this man's anger by telling him that his strain was mental—and was unnecessary.

"Can I tell that to the landlord?" he barked explosively.

"Have you had your breakfast this morning?" I asked.

"Yes, I have, but what has that to do with my problem?"

"You're feeling comfortable at this moment, are you?" I ventured as the expression on his face became more and more puzzled.

"Yes, but I don't know what you're driving at," he replied with his voice getting higher and higher.

"You admitted you are feeling comfortable at this moment, which indicates that your mental strain is not caused by something which is happening now, but through fear of that which might happen in the future," I admonished cautiously.

He readily admitted I was right, but added:

"I am under a strain due to what might happen, but stopping worry will not pay the landlord. What am I to do?"

"What are you doing now to ease your situation?" I asked.

"What can I do? I am so worried I can't get a job or do anything which will help," he moaned.

"Suppose you were given time to re-establish yourself before this landslide comes down on your head, what would you do?" I resumed thoughtfully.

Thinking I was going to get some sort of reprieve for him, he knitted his brow and appeared to be doing some serious thinking. He came up with a most worthy idea; one which I knew would work.

"Now then, you go to your landlord and tell him of your plan. Let him see your sincerity and I feel certain he will play ball with you," I suggested tactfully.

At first my visitor resented the idea but, as we talked about it, he agreed that it was well worth trying.

He went to his landlord, and to his surprise the landlord complimented him on the idea and told him to go ahead and put it into effect.

That man's problem ceased to be a problem,—and he proved my point that his state of mind when he first came to me was unnecessary and destructive.

A woman came to me greatly upset over the fact that her husband was about to leave her and wanted a divorce. She was so upset her thinking was barely coherent.

I told her that her present mental state was unnecessary and thought for a moment I was going to get my face slapped.

Nothing at all was happening to her at the moment. This certainly indicated that her mental state was due entirely to what might happen in the future because of what had happened in the past.

"What are you doing to correct your condition?" I asked.

She admitted that about all she was doing was living in misery, awaiting the day when her husband would leave.

I urged her to spend her time in making herself the kind of wife a man would like. Instead of presenting herself as a picture of gloom, she should discipline herself to be radiantly alive and cheerful.

At first she thought of many reasons why she should not give in and be sweet to him, but as we talked she realized that my suggestion could easily prove to be the solution.

My advice was accepted and followed, with the result that this couple is now most happy and all thoughts of divorce have vanished.

You see? The state of mind this woman was in, when first coming to me was unnecessary.

If your mind is troubled, think of your condition as it is at the moment; right now in this infinitesimal space of time we call the present. You are most likely to find that nothing is happening at the moment which could be disturbing, but that your strain is due to a combination of past circumstances and fear of the future.

When just a young man, I was told that my services were no longer required at the place where I had been working. I was given two weeks notice.

On my way home that evening, my mind was in a turmoil. My mental pictures were all dismal. I had no money saved up; what would I do? Pictures of eviction and even hunger crossed my mind. After allowing myself to become as miserable as possible, I turned my thoughts to the positive side of the picture.

"I have two weeks before my salary ends," I thought. "I will go out and get myself a better job." This I did. I landed a job I liked more than the one I had—and at a third more salary.

I might close this portion of this chapter with the thought: *Keep your present happily occupied in carrying out your plans for the future.*

Anticipation

This entire book, up to this point, has been devoted to *your* future and how to have a future of *your own* making

You have learned about objectives—both major and minor— and how to attain them.

You have taken steps toward the establishment of a new standard of living, built around your new life pattern. Thoughts herein expressed are not so much repetition as they are summation; intended not only to fix them in your mind—but to stimulate action during the only time you will ever have—*now*.

A constructive mind is a happy mind. When you are marching forward toward your objective, your mind is happy. At the end of the day you enjoy your period of rest and relaxation because you feel you have earned it. You sleep peacefully without a troubled mind, and awaken in the morning ready and anxious to start another day of constructive activity.

Train yourself to be orderly and systematic. It will astonish you to find how much more work you will do and with less exertion.

"I have so many things to do, I become frustrated," said a man who wanted help. This chap admitted that when he would think of everything he had to do, it would be hard for him to concentrate on any one thing.

"How many things do you have to do?" I inquired, sympathetically.

"Gosh, I don't know. I just haven't counted them," he replied.

I handed him a sheet of paper and a pencil and suggested that he write down all of the jobs he had ahead of him. When the list was completed, it contained so few items, he felt sure he must have overlooked several. But, think as he did, he could add no more to the list.

"Take this list and rearrange the items in the order of their importance," I advised, "and keep it ever before you. As you complete a job, cross it off the list. Should new jobs come before completing these, add them to the list."

Later I was told that he is accomplishing far more than he did before—and enjoying every bit of it.

Most fatigue is mental. We get tired because we expect to get tired. A person will arise in the morning and, when he thinks of the many things he has to do during the day, he gets tired in anticipation of the fatigue he is sure will come.

Many people will start the day by doing all of the easy things first. This person will not enjoy what he is doing because his mind is on the difficult things to come. He tires quickly because by the time he has completed the simpler jobs he has brought on a psychosomatic fatigue through just thinking about the difficult jobs.

When one starts his day by doing the harder jobs first, he

will find that they are not as hard as he anticipated, because he is starting when his mind and body are fresh. Also, while on the harder jobs, his mind is on the easy ones to follow which gives him something pleasant to think about, in contrast to his thoughts when starting with the easy jobs.

Prevent yourself from developing a "hard job" consciousness. Instead of holding to the thought "This job will be difficult and trying," see it as a task you'll enjoy and that you are thoroughly capable of doing quickly and without great effort.

• • • • •

This chapter brings to a close the book designed to give you an I WILL consciousness; that state of mind where you will back your resolutions with determination—and action.

There is not a single thought in this book which has not been proved; which is not being proved; and which will not be proved time and time again.

As monumental as the promises made to you have been, there is not one of them which cannot be carried through to fulfillment. Your future is like the clay in the hands of the sculptor, you can do with it as you will.

And you *will* make your future a glorious one. Were you not sincere, you would never see these words because you would have closed your book long ere this.

Take Your First Step Now!

You have learned that you can never do anything except in the now—the present. Take your first step now. It may be nothing more than writing down your major objective—and breaking it down into its minor objectives.

After you have taken your first step, and in your spare time— begin reading the book all over again. Have a red pencil with you and use it to mark wherever you wish. Underline every thought which seemed intended for you. This means that in the future—everytime you open the book—a key thought will jump out at you as a reminder of the things you *will* do.

Here's another suggestion and one which may seem strange to you. Ordinarily one is advised to keep his plans secret and there are times when this is advisable. In your case—I will advise differently.

Talk about your future! If you have a family, tell your mate about the new vistas you see ahead and which will be yours. Emphasize the fact that from this day onward things will begin to happen to make a reality of those things which heretofore were thought of as idle dreams.

Talk about your journey! Tell about the exciting stations you visited and what they will mean to you.

Tell your close friend—with marked enthusiasm—about your new life pattern. Assure them that it is not wishful thinking, but that you have everything you need to make your objectives realities, and that you're already on your way.

Every time you have a chance to peer into a mirror, notice the new expression which is coming to your face. You will be able to actually see your growth.

Soon your friends will begin asking you what has happened; you look so much better than you did and, yes, younger. Because once your cares are converted into enthusiastic constructive action thoughts, you do become younger.

•   •   •   •   •

The pages which follow—Modus Operandi—contain specific rules for handling specific objectives. Keep them always handy for future reference. These rules will add still more fun to your doing.

MODUS OPERANDI

How and Why the Mind Can Make You Rich

If you have a mind somewhat similar to mine, you will welcome this chapter—and profit greatly by it.

I was born with an inquisitive mind. The words *how* and *why* are always uppermost in my thinking.

When I was first learning to drive an automobile—about 1915—all gear shifting was done with a "wobble stick" which came through the floor; I was not contented to merely know that by placing the lever in one position you would be in first gear, another position would give you second gear, and so on. I wanted to see what happened when you moved the lever; so I removed the cover from the transmission box and watched how the gear ratios changed with each movement of the shift lever.

When I first started studying people, I was not happy to merely know that some people had a faculty of making and accumulating wealth, while others seemed to fail in every undertaking. I wanted to know why; I wanted to know why they are as they are. I wanted to know if a person could change from a ne'er-do-well to an individual of affluence or if his mind was fixed like his bone structure and height.

Everything given in this book is based upon principles which have been proved, are being proved and will be proved time and time again.

I hope you are the inquisitive type. If you are, this chapter will convince you beyond a shadow of a doubt that these principles will not only work for the other fellow—but will work for you.

I have always enjoyed watching magicians practice their feats of legerdemain. There was one trick I saw performed which seemed beyond comprehension. One day, a magician I had become acquainted with exposed the trick. It was so downright simple—a child of 12 could perform it after 5 minutes instruction.

To say that an individual who has gone through life a failure can, through following a prescribed mental regimen, change to an outstanding success seems a bit difficult to believe. But, if you understand *how* and *why*—a change of your mental pattern will bring about such a transformation, you will not be practicing any form of black magic, but will be making use of natural mental laws.

Hypnosis—Post Hypnosis—Self-Hypnosis

In order to help you gain a better insight to the mind and how it operates, I wish to discuss, briefly, hypnosis, post hypnosis and self-hypnosis.

Around the turn of the century, it might have been unwise to mention anything about hypnotism. At that time public opinion was quite evenly divided; some people believing it to be allied with magic; others were afraid of it.

Whether you know it or not, every individual is daily being affected by hypnosis—post hypnosis—and self-hypnosis.

Webster defines hypnotism as being: "A state resembling normal sleep, differing in being induced by the suggestions and operations of the hypnotizer, with whom the hypnotized subject remains in rapport, responsive to his suggestions." Please note the preciseness of this definition. It does not, in any way, cast any reflection on the authenticity of hypnotism.

Hypnotism is based on the fact that though the conscious mind can sleep, the subconscious mind is awake 24 hours of every day.

A hypnotist creates induced sleep, then talks to the subconscious mind—which never sleeps.

The subconscious mind—when under hypnosis—will accept

all suggestions it wants to accept. One will never accept suggestions contrary to his principles or beliefs, but he will accept suggestions in keeping with his desires.

As an illustration: I once hypnotized a youth who was so timid he could not talk to three people at a time without becoming tongue-tied. After I had induced hypnotic sleep I told him he was a great orator. I told him he was standing on the platform in a crowded auditorium and that he was prepared and ready to give a lecture. I suggested a subject.

For several minutes that young man stood there and, with perfect poise, well chosen words, and sound logic, gave a talk anyone would enjoy hearing. All of that, mind you, coming from a very timid boy.

There is not a timid person who does not wish he could talk before others without fear or hesitation; so a suggestion to one to the effect that he is a great orator will be readily accepted.

Here is a little known fact. Actually, the hypnotist does not hypnotize the subject; the subject hypnotizes himself. For example: While creating induced hypnotic sleep, the operator will stand in front of the subject and make such suggestions as: "You're getting sleepy. Your eyelids are getting heavy. Your vision is getting dim, etc." In time the eyes of the subject will begin to blink and before long he will bow his head and be off in slumberland. While in a state of induced hypnotic sleep, he responds to nothing except the voice of the operator.

For while the hypnotist is making the statement: "You're getting sleepy," in reality, the subject is thinking: "I'm getting sleepy. My eyelids are getting heavy."

It is not necessary to be hypnotized in order to be affected by suggestion. If I should say to you: "There was a worm in that apple you just ate," even though I was telling an untruth, you would most likely become ill. You would become ill through the suggestion which you believed.

In an office, three of the young men employees decided to try a psychological experiment with one of the girls. When the selected girl arrived in the morning, one of the men approached her and said: "You must be ill. You are not looking a bit well."

"I feel all right," she replied without hesitation—but the thought had been planted.

A bit later, one of the other boys saw her and made the same remark. By this time, the girl did feel a little bit on the ill side.

The third man commented on the way she looked. By noon that girl was so ill she had to go home. She had accepted suggestions which she believed.

In the afternoon, the boys, feeling repentant, 'phoned this girl and told her it was all a hoax. She became well immediately and returned to the office.

If you're taking a new job and someone should tell you that you'll never make good in it, should you believe that person, it is quite probable you will fail. You have been affected through the law of suggestion.

The late Dr. John Schindler pointed out that 70 per cent of all ailments were psychosomatic.* This means that 7 out of 10 ailments have their origin in mind. If this percentage of people can become ill through the mind—it is safe to conclude that a large percentage of physical ailments can be corrected through a change in thinking.

At one time in New York City, a certain doctor suddenly gained quite a reputation for his remarkable cures. He filled his own prescriptions.

On one occasion, I accompanied a young lady to this doctor's office so that he could treat her for a condition which had been causing considerable suffering.

The doctor, in a most professional way, felt her pulse, listened to her heart, etc. Then, after asking many questions, left for his room where he could prepare the prescription. It so happened, where my chair was placed, I could see into the prescription room of the doctor. I saw him remove a box from the shelf—and from it scooped up enough small white tablets to fill two bottles. He labeled the bottles #1 and #2. Remember both bottles were filled from the same box.

He then handed these bottles to the patient and gave her most elaborate directions as to when and how to take them. She should take pill #1 before each meal, and #2 just before retiring. These pills, which I found out to be nothing but com-

---

* John A. Schindler, M.D., *How to Live 365 Days a Year.* (Englewood Cliffs, N.J.: Prentice-Hall, Inc., 1954.)

pressed sugar, were doing much good for patients. But it was not the sugar which helped, it was the *belief* they would help. In other words, the patients were helped through a principle of hypnosis: the law of suggestion.

To give an idea of the potency of hypnotic suggestion: I have seen dental patients have teeth extracted—without the slightest discomfort—when under hypnosis. Minor surgical operations have been performed while the patients were under hypnosis.

Post hypnosis pertains to suggestions made to a subject while under hypnosis—and which are carried out at a later date.

For example: A hypnotist might say to a boy while under hypnosis: "Each morning you will awaken early and have an impulse to get up and dress so that you will have plenty of time for your breakfast and not be late to school." Or, the boy might be told he will enjoy his arithmetic—and, as a result of his interest in the subject, will get high marks in school. These are post hypnotic suggestions.

Self-Hypnosis is, just as the name implies, a state of hypnosis which one consciously brings on himself. Some have demonstrated that, through the principles of self-hypnosis, they can exert certain influences in their beings, and in their affairs.

All of us are constantly being influenced through the power of suggestion, either for good or for bad. Some might associate this phenomena with hypnology, but I would rather think of it as the power of suggestion.

In the natural flow of our thoughts are many undirected suggestions which can react for our good or bad depending on their nature.

Undirected suggestions might be referred to as auto-suggestion; those which we initiate for a specific reaction are conscious auto-suggestions.

In this work I am particularly interested in encouraging the use of conscious auto-suggestion as it pertains to self-improvement and well being. You will find it to be a certain means of conquering and controlling one's self. Self-mastery is manhood in its glory. "He that is slow to anger is better than the mighty; and he that ruleth his spirit better than he that taketh a city." (Prov. 16:32.)

Please do not misunderstand me. When I say we will use the principles of conscious auto-suggestion, I am in no way implying that we will merely be "kidding" ourselves. We will be employing sound psychological principles. But, when you fully comprehend why we are as we are, you will understand how downright simple it will be to change ourselves in any desired way.

You are what you think you are! The *you* of today is the composite of all of the thought patterns established in your mind since babyhood. As referred to earlier in this work, if you are timid it is because, as a small child, you accepted the thought that you were timid. And you'll be timid just as long as you hold to the thought that you are a timid person.

In nearly all cases, when a person is constantly complaining of aches and pains, he is reflecting a condition established in his mind when he was very small. Throughout his life he holds on to the thought that he is not up to par—that he cannot stand much hard work, etc.

Each time a person holds such a thought, whether he knows it or not, is using a principle of auto-suggestion.

Fatigue is often encouraged through a principle of auto-suggestion. If one has much work to do—especially work he is not too fond of doing—he will bring on fatigue much earlier than necessary, because he has been expecting to get tired.

"I just dread going to bed because I know I will not go to sleep." Nothing could be more closely related to auto-suggestion than statements of this kind. One, through such a suggestion, is literally instructing his subconscious mind to keep him awake.

Coffee, unless exceptionally strong, will lose its stimulating effect about 2 hours after drinking it. Many people will hesitate to drink coffee with a 6 o'clock dinner, being sure it will keep them awake. They do stay awake but it was not the coffee which kept them awake. It was the suggestion they imposed upon themselves at the time they drank the coffee.

Have you ever given yourself instructions to wake up at a certain time in the morning? You do wake up, don't you? That is conscious auto-suggestion.

Do you know that a bad memory, in most cases, is due to the suggestions you make to yourself? Every time you say: "I have a bad memory," you're making it more real. The next time you want to remember something, give yourself a *positive* suggestion. Say: "I'll think of it in a minute," and you will.

If you have been creating a bad memory by holding the thought you have a bad memory, begin saying to yourself: "I have a good memory!" Say it many times and soon there will be a good memory pattern established in your mind. And it will develop through the principles of conscious self-suggestion.

In an earlier chapter, I told you about the group of salesmen I met with each Monday morning and had them start their days with the thought: "I Am a great Salesman!" They did improve their salesmanship—materially—and it was through a principle of conscious self-suggestion.

Some time ago one of the popular magazines told the story of an experiment tried with a sufferer of hay fever. A vase of artificial flowers was placed in this person's room, flowers of the type which normally aggravated his malady. His eyes started watering; his nose began to run. Through self-suggestion he began suffering all the ill effects of hay fever.

A woman confined in a hospital after a serious operation could not drop off to sleep at night unless the doctor gave her a narcotic. The doctor feared that to keep this up too long would make her dependent upon the drug.

When he tried to stop administering the drug, she begged for it, claiming she could not go to sleep with the pain she had. The doctor filled the hypodermic needle with nothing but warm water and gave her the injection. Soon she dropped off into peaceful sleep. This patient did not know it—but the sleep was brought on through self-suggestion.

Much of the pain experienced in a dental chair is self-induced through the principles of self-suggestion. For hours—and sometimes days—a person will dread going to his dentist, *knowing* how much he will be hurt. When the needle is inserted in his gums, he squirms and groans, but in reality the pain is far less severe than the patient makes it out to be.

All people are constantly using the principles of *post hypnosis;* that condition whereby we make the suggestion to ourselves and act upon it later.

One time I was leaving New York on a transcontinental motor trip at the same time a friend of mine was doing like-wise. I looked forward to the trip because I knew every mile of it would be enjoyable. The other fellow dreaded his trip. He knew it would be tiresome and monotonous. We met in San Francisco a few weeks later and compared notes on our trips. Both of us had proved to be good prophets. I had a wonderful trip. His was boring and tiresome. Each of us had set our subconscious patterns before leaving, with the results already mentioned. This was post hypnosis in action. Before leaving we had accepted the suggestions which were acted upon later.

Although there is a physiological reason for many cases of sea-sickness, it is true that most people become seasick because they expect to become seasick. In other words, when beginning a cruise, they just *know* they will be seasick.

●　　●　　●　　●　　●

I have used these pages in talking about hypnotism, suggestion, self-suggestion and auto-suggestion so that you will understand why all of the principles given in this book will be effective. There should no longer be any mystery attached to self-improvement.

You will follow the suggestions given because you know they *will* work—and you know *why* they will work.

I want you to understand the potency of suggestion. I want you to guard every thought you express to others. I want you to guard every thought you apply to yourselves.

"Charity begins at home," is a truism. It can also be said that the place to begin practicing the use of positive suggestions is the home.

Be extremely careful with your children. The thoughtless remarks you make today might be felt throughout the life of the child.

Never refer to the child as being bad. Through suggestion,

you are implanting a "bad child" seed in the subconscious mind of the child. If you must correct the young one, instead of referring to him as being bad, say something such as: "Good boys do not do that." You see? You are comparing the child with good instead of bad.

Husband and wives should be extremely careful in the way they speak to each other regarding looks and age.

"You're not as young as you used to be," and such remarks, will give one a consciousness of age, which will put the processes of Nature to work to hasten age.

At the time of writing this, I have just passed my 25th wedding anniversary. For me to say that my wife looks about as young today as she did when we were married might reflect the oft said remark that "love is blind." But the frequency with which I hear that remark from people who have known us for 25 years leads me to believe my eyes are not deceiving me.

In talking to her, I never refer to age in any way except to think in terms of youth. To me she is my sweet young wife and I always refer to her as such. She never gives any thought to herself as being anything but "my young wife."

I like to brag about *my* age. I enjoy seeing the expression on the faces of others when I tell them I am past the three score years and ten and that, according to the scriptures, I am living on borrowed time. Regardless of my chronological age, I am not old. I am not old because I have never allowed myself to think in terms of age. My mind is keen and alert; I have a spring in my step; my bodily organs are all functioning as they should function. I am *not* bragging. I am merely telling you what can happen when you discipline yourself to think in terms of youth and vigorous health.

•   •   •   •   •

The final chapter gives specific formulas for specific objectives. Although suggested affirmations are given, do not feel you must follow these word for word. They are to be considered more as models. You will quickly learn how to compose your own.

I have not given all objectives by any means. I might not have touched upon yours at all—but, studying those given, you will be able to create the exact phraseology to meet your specific objective.

In writing your affirmations, there is a warning I must give you. Do not use what psychologists refer to as a reverse negative. There are times when a positive thought can be negative in its effect.

For example: I might say: "Do not think of that lamp!" I may warn you time and time again to take your mind completely off of the lamp. And, you know, the more I make the statement, the more you will think of the lamp, even though you try to do otherwise. I am focusing attention on the lamp. But, if I should say something about a chair, I have then taken your mind away from the lamp.

So a good formula to follow is: *Concentrate on the condition you want, not the one you are trying to dispose of.*

You were told in a previous chapter that our lives are made up of habits.

Begin forming new life habits. From now on your thinking is to be positive—constructive. You will slip many times at first, but do not become discouraged. It is so natural to think negatively that you will, many times, catch yourself holding to a negative thought. Even the fact that you will be aware of your waning negative thinking will indicate that you are improving. And, each time you discover yourself thinking in a negative way, you will become that much more conscious of your changing trend of thought.

SPECIFIC FORMULAS
FOR SPECIFIC OBJECTIVES

The following pages give suggested affirmations covering many objectives. They are arranged alphabetically, not necessarily in the order of their importance.

When working on an objective, it is a good idea to copy the affirmation on a small card and carry it with you. Repeat it time and time again; the first thing in the morning—whenever you think of it during the day—and several times before retiring.

Do not repeat it mechanically, but as a specific instruction to your subconscious mind; *knowing* it will come to pass.

If you had an employee and you wanted him to do a certain thing for you, you would give the necessary instructions and you know, without doubt, he will carry them out.

The affirmations herein contained are to be given to the most faithful servant you will ever have. Your subconscious mind *will* follow your instructions if properly given.

From time to time you will have objectives other than those included in the following pages. You can take any one of these and modify it to fit your circumstances—or create entirely new ones. Be careful, of course, to write it so that it will apply to the conditions you want, not the one you're trying to overcome.

In preparing this book for you, I have practiced what I preach. I directed my subconscious mind to guide me in writing the most powerful self-help book within my capabilities. As I re-read it, I feel my instructions have been carried out.

AUTOMOBILE

Suppose you have been driving a car which has seen its best days, and you feel you have reached the point where you want one of the new, high-powered cars.

At the moment your circumstances might not be such that you can nonchalantly walk in a showroom and buy a car as readily as you would pick up a can of beans in your supermarket.

First decide on the car you want. Visit automobile row and look them over. Do not look at a car with a wish on your lips, because a wish expresses a doubt. You do not wish for things you know you can have, do you?

After you have made your selection, then go to work in getting your faithful subconscious mind on the job. From early morning until you retire at night, implant in your mind the thought:

> *"I will be guided in my thoughts and actions to do the things which will pave the way to bring the selected automobile into my possession, without financial stress of any kind."*

Your thoughts will begin to flow. Ideas will come to you as to how you might make the best kind of a deal on the car. Avenues will open up whereby you will obtain the necessary money for payments without adding any burden to you.

A BUSINESS OF YOUR OWN

A large percentage of men and women aspire to some day be in business for themselves. This might be true with you. If your decision—while on our fabulous journey—was to head a business bearing your name, the following affirmation will condition your subconscious mind so that there will be no doubt at all as to the attainment of your objective.

Remember! This and other affirmations will not cause your objective to materialize by itself—like a magician pulling a rabbit out of his hat. Many steps must be followed to make your objective a reality.

These affirmations will guide you in your thinking so that you will march resolutely onward toward your objective with a happy, enthusiastic mind, free from doubtful worry.

The following suggestion to your subconscious mind is basic. Add to it any thoughts which will make it apply to your specific objective.

> *"I am being guided in my thoughts and actions in the direction of establishing a business of my own. I am fully capable of managing a business of my own. I will climb to success because my motives are unselfish. My success will enable me to do more for others."*

BETTER HEALTH

Let me first say, *emphatically,* do not attempt to be your own doctor. Everyone should have regular physical check-ups and, if any ailment is discovered, it should be treated by the man who has dedicated his life to save lives, your doctor.

Many cases, however, are psychosomatic: ailments resulting from a mind filled with fears regarding illness—and death.

A happy, positive thinking mind is conducive to good health.

Parents, due to their anxiety to keep their children well, very frequently develop a mental pattern of fear of illness in the young minds. The children then grow into adulthood with attention focused on ailments rather than robust health.

Everyone should create within his mind an image of health. He should always be thinking of himself as enjoying good health, instead of worrying about the various physical conditions which could develop.

To establish a health pattern within your mind, hold to a thought, such as:

> *"My health is constantly improving because I am guided to think in terms of health and strength and vitality. I will be led to do the things which will assist Nature in giving me a body of radiant health."*

DEVELOPING THE POWERS OF CONCENTRATION

Most people would resent being called a "scatter-brain," yet most people are, to a certain extent, scatter-brains.

Do not worry! This is not an indication that one's brain is affected or that he may end up in a mental institution.

Lacking the powers of mental concentration merely shows that one has formed bad mental habits. Permitting all sorts of extraneous thoughts to enter your mind takes away your ability to concentrate at will. But, just as we can strengthen our muscles through proper exercise, so too can one develop his powers of concentration through a proper routine of mental exercise.

Concentration is covered in an earlier chapter of this book. If you are in earnest in developing your powers of concentration, instead of thinking of yourself as one who cannot concentrate, build a new thought pattern with a suggestion, such as:

"I am blessed with great powers of mental concentration. I can hold my thoughts on a single idea until I elect to discharge it from my mind."

DOMESTIC HARMONY

Unless a person is happy in his home life, he will not be happy anywhere.

Domestic inharmony is often caused by boredom. Husbands and wives do not keep their interests alive and, believe it or not, (subconsciously) bickering, nagging, growling, fighting, give the couple something to do.

Rarely will you encounter domestic inharmony when the path is onward and upward and both mates are devoted to constructive thinking.

Husbands and wives should not blame each other for faults. Blame yourself. Ask yourself: "What can I do to make this marriage an outstanding success?"

If each party will devote his or her life in doing everything possible to make the other happy—without thought of what might be done in return—you know as well as I do that happiness will result.

My responsibility toward you would not be complete if I did not suggest a means of making your home life ideally happy. Success in your business or job—with an unhappy home—would give you a definitely unbalanced life.

The step toward a happier home life is to implant in your mind a thought such as:

> *"I am guided to give full expression of my love for my mate. I am at all times prompted to do the things which will give the greatest happiness, thereby assuring my own happiness."*

OVERCOMING HABITS

Think of yourself as being a mind with a body; not a body with a mind. When you fully realize that your body is merely a utility for the mind, you will no longer permit your body to dictate to you as to what you shall and shall not do.

If you have a habit which is proving too costly to you; costly not only from the standpoint of cost, but from the damage it does to your physical being, know that through your self-mastery you can easily conquer the habit.

Instead of holding the thought that you are a slave to the habit—and cannot correct it—build on a thought, such as:

> *"I have full control over my tastes and desires. I do those things which promote my well being and refrain from doing things which will in any way affect my health and financial standing."*

HAPPINESS

As much as one might yearn for happiness, it is gratifying to know that it is within the reach of all of us, because happiness comes from within. It is not an external condition. Our happiness is not contingent upon people or things, but rather upon our attitude toward people and things.

Our first station on the big journey we recently completed was named happiness. At that station you learned that, to be happy, one needs to give expression to the happiness he has within.

To help you establish a mental pattern of happiness, I suggest that you make the following affirmation a permanent part of your consciousness:

"I am happy. I am happy because of my good health. I am happy because my path in life leads onward and upward. I am happy because of my ability to master conditions instead of being mastered by them. I am happy."

A HOME OF YOUR OWN

To own a piece of the earth on which you live, with a comfortable home located on it, is the objective of nearly everyone.

As you raised your standards of living, undoubtedly a new, modern home was placed high on your list of objectives.

This can become a reality just as fast as you wish to make it so. The moment you take the first steps toward bringing your objective into being, you will have started the forces of Nature working for you—and things will begin to happen.

Remember what you already learned regarding being specific. Do not merely have as an objective a new home, but decide what kind of a home—and where it will be located. And, you must become "new home" conscious. Just take it for granted that soon you'll be moving into the home of your dreams.

To help you gain that "new home" consciousness, keep ever before you a thought, such as:

"I will be guided in my thoughts and actions toward the acquiring of a new home. I will locate just the property I want, at a price, and with terms, which will be exactly as I want them."

SECURING A BETTER JOB

In Dr. Russell Conwell's masterpiece *Acres of Diamonds,* he points out that many people are searching for that which they already have. Many job holders are seeking better jobs without realizing the opportunities right under their feet.

The one with a creative mind can often make of his present job a better one which will be more pleasant and profitable. This thought is advanced with the suggestion that, before seeking another job, you thoroughly evaluate the one you have to make certain you are not missing any opportunities for advancement.

Sometimes, by studying your job, you will find ways of doing your work better, faster, or more economically. And remember, the more valuable you make your services to your employer, the more your employer will do to keep you happy.

In looking for a better job—either through promotion with your present company or with another company—establish in your mind a "better job" consciousness.

The following suggestion, repeated many, many times, will prove of material help.

> *"I am being guided in my thoughts and actions to do everything necessary to enable me to gain a substantial promotion with the company I am now with, or to have my outstanding work recognized by an employer who will properly compensate me for my worth."*

PROBLEMS, AND HOW TO OVERCOME THEM

Problems, when faced by the one with the right mental attitude, are not really problems at all. Because he can readily find a solution to them, they actually add interest to one's day.

If you are a card player, when you get a bad hand of cards, you do not consider that Fate is against you and begin feeling sorry for yourself. No! You consider the bad hand as a challenge, and you use every bit of knowledge you have in trying to play the hand so that it will be a winning one. When you win with such a hand, the satisfaction is far greater than when you win with a good hand.

To give you full mastery over your problems, build on an affirmative thought, such as:

"I am at peace with myself and the world. Problems facing me are not disturbing because I have made contact with my true source of intelligence and power. I am guided to do the right thing at the right time."

PUBLIC SPEAKING

The words "Public Speaking" are frightening to most people. They bring mental pictures of standing on a platform, knees trembling and tongue-tied, while the audience laughs.

And the longer you hold to such a mental picture, the more difficult it will be to stand on a platform and give a lecture.

If you realize that the intelligence of an audience is no greater than the intelligence of a single individual—and that you would not hesitate to talk to a single individual—then you will have no difficulty at all talking before the public. In fact, you will quickly reach the point where you will enjoy public speaking.

Should you be scheduled to give a talk (and now, with your new life pattern, this will be often) impress your mind with this truth:

"I truly love people and enjoy talking to them. I have perfect poise when on a platform, because I know I am liked by those who will listen. My thoughts will flow freely and, with a firm clear voice, I will impress my listeners."

SALESMANSHIP!

Sixty per cent of all people are dependent, either directly or indirectly, on salesmanship for a livelihood.

Even though you might not be engaged as a salesman, one often employs the principles of salesmanship. Any time you are attempting any kind of persuasion, you are using salesmanship.

If you are engaged as a salesman, and travelling from one prospect to another, instead of making yourself frustrated by wondering what kind of a reception you will get, put the principles of auto-suggestion to work for you.

With a firm step and your chest and chin out, declare to yourself, knowingly:

> *"I Am a Great Salesman. When talking to a prospect I am guided as to what to say and how to say it, so that I will be successful in gaining his interest in that which I am selling."*

SELF-MASTERY

The essence of this entire book is self-mastery. Self-mastery does not mean the mastery of body; it means the mastery of mind, because, without mind, the body would be inanimate.

We have learned that success and happiness are a matter of consciousness; that we first think in terms of success before we manifest success.

It would appear then, that to change our conditions we must change our attitude toward them.

So much has been given throughout this book regarding consciousness, awareness—and attitude, an affirmation on this subject might be unnecessary.

However, here is an affirmation for self-mastery in the event you should, at times, feel the need of augmenting the self-mastery spirit you already have.

> *"I am master of my being. I am master of the thoughts I am thinking and the things I am doing. Through my self-mastery, my path leads constantly onward and upward."*

TIMIDITY

Overcoming timidity is a simple matter if you will accept it as such. This statement may be a bit hard to believe at first, because timidity, throughout a lifetime, will cause so much mental suffering. It seems too good to be true that simple relief is at hand. But it is!

Overcoming timidity is largely a matter of changing your mind. For years you have been adding to your timidity through the thoughts of timidity you have been holding, each one making your condition more apparent.

To overcome timidity all that is necessary is to build up a consciousness just the reverse of the one you have. (This might not apply to you—if not, please ignore it.)

Whether you are timid or not, it will prove of material help to repeat this statement, slowly and thoughtfully, a number of times, morning and night:

> *"I love all of humanity. I enjoy being with people. I like to converse with people. It gives me happiness to make others happy."*

WORRY, AND HOW TO OVERCOME IT

My best definition of worry is: "Maintaining mental pictures of things you do not want." Throughout this book you have been building mental pictures of things you do want.

If worry is focused on a disturbing problem, to merely suggest that you forget it would probably prove more disastrous than the worry. Worry, at least, indicates cognizance of the existence of a problem. What must be done, therefore, is to find a constructive substitute for the worry—something which will solve the problem instead of permitting it to remain as a mental bugaboo.

The following affirmation will not only allay the worry but will bring into consciousness constructive thoughts which will provide the means to prevent the worry.

> *"My mind is free from worry because I am in direct contact with the source of power and intelligence which enables me to dissolve the cause of the worry. My subconscious mind will direct me in thought and in action toward the elimination of my worries."*

HOW TO BECOME A WRITER

"I would like to be a writer—but I know I could never be one," explained a woman who had come to me for counsel.

"Have you ever tried to write?" I asked politely.

"What's the use? I haven't any talent in that direction," she replied with definite conviction.

For a solid hour, I preached to this girl, proving to her that with her attitude she was blocking all possibility of writing.

I gave her a formula to follow; a suggestion based on auto-suggestion, without telling her so; and within seven months from the time she visited me, she had a story accepted and now follows writing as a career.

Here is the affirmation I gave to her and which you might like to use, if your mind ever turns toward the art of writing:

> *"I enjoy writing and can write well because my powers of imagination are great, and I have the ability to express myself in writing in a simple, understandable and interesting manner. When writing my thoughts flow freely and without effort. I am a good writer."*

FINAL!

No matter what it is you want to do, give yourself a reputation for being able to do it, and the best way to give yourself such a reputation is through carefully worded affirmations.

Start the day with such thoughts as: *"This will be a happy day. It will be a day of great accomplishment."*

Before retiring at night, put yourself in the proper frame of mind with such thoughts as: *"I am looking forward to my bed. It will be a pleasure to remove my clothing and thoroughly relaxing in a fine, comfortable bed. I will go to sleep easily—and will sleep peacefully."*

Know that your conscious mind is master; your subconscious mind is your servant. It will do just as you instruct it to do. If you hold negative thoughts, you are giving your subconscious mind definite instructions to make your thoughts realities.

If you hold positive, constructive thoughts, the reverse will be true. You will get positive results.

• • • • •

I have enjoyed my journey with you—tremendously.

A PERSONAL WORD FROM MELVIN POWERS, PUBLISHER, WILSHIRE BOOK COMPANY

My goal is to publish interesting, informative, and inspirational books. You can help me to accomplish this by sending me your answers to the following questions:

Did you enjoy reading this book? Why?

What ideas in the book impressed you most? Have you applied them to your daily life? How?

Is there a chapter that could serve as a theme for an entire book? Explain.

Would you like to read similar books? What additional information would you like them to contain?

If you have an idea for a book, I would welcome discussing it with you. If you have a manuscript in progress, write or call me concerning possible publication.

Melvin Powers
12015 Sherman Road
North Hollywood, California 91605

(818) 765-8579

MELVIN POWERS SELF-IMPROVEMENT LIBRARY

ASTROLOGY

____ ASTROLOGY: HOW TO CHART YOUR HOROSCOPE *Max Heindel*	5.00
____ ASTROLOGY AND SEXUAL ANALYSIS *Morris C. Goodman*	5.00
____ ASTROLOGY AND YOU *Carroll Righter*	5.00
____ ASTROLOGY MADE EASY *Astarte*	5.00
____ ASTROLOGY, ROMANCE, YOU AND THE STARS *Anthony Norvell*	5.00
____ MY WORLD OF ASTROLOGY *Sydney Omarr*	7.00
____ THOUGHT DIAL *Sydney Omarr*	7.00
____ WHAT THE STARS REVEAL ABOUT THE MEN IN YOUR LIFE *Thelma White*	3.00

BRIDGE

____ BRIDGE BIDDING MADE EASY *Edwin B. Kantar*	10.00
____ BRIDGE CONVENTIONS *Edwin B. Kantar*	10.00
____ COMPETITIVE BIDDING IN MODERN BRIDGE *Edgar Kaplan*	7.00
____ DEFENSIVE BRIDGE PLAY COMPLETE *Edwin B. Kantar*	15.00
____ GAMESMAN BRIDGE—PLAY BETTER WITH KANTAR *Edwin B. Kantar*	7.00
____ HOW TO IMPROVE YOUR BRIDGE *Alfred Sheinwold*	7.00
____ IMPROVING YOUR BIDDING SKILLS *Edwin B. Kantar*	7.00
____ INTRODUCTION TO DECLARER'S PLAY *Edwin B. Kantar*	7.00
____ INTRODUCTION TO DEFENDER'S PLAY *Edwin B. Kantar*	7.00
____ KANTAR FOR THE DEFENSE *Edwin B. Kantar*	7.00
____ KANTAR FOR THE DEFENSE VOLUME 2 *Edwin B. Kantar*	7.00
____ TEST YOUR BRIDGE PLAY *Edwin B. Kantar*	7.00
____ VOLUME 2—TEST YOUR BRIDGE PLAY *Edwin B. Kantar*	7.00
____ WINNING DECLARER PLAY *Dorothy Hayden Truscott*	7.00

BUSINESS, STUDY & REFERENCE

____ BRAINSTORMING *Charles Clark*	7.00
____ CONVERSATION MADE EASY *Elliot Russell*	5.00
____ EXAM SECRET *Dennis B. Jackson*	5.00
____ FIX-IT BOOK *Arthur Symons*	2.00
____ HOW TO DEVELOP A BETTER SPEAKING VOICE *M. Hellier*	4.00
____ HOW TO SAVE 50% ON GAS & CAR EXPENSES *Ken Stansbie*	5.00
____ HOW TO SELF-PUBLISH YOUR BOOK & MAKE IT A BEST SELLER *Melvin Powers*	20.00
____ INCREASE YOUR LEARNING POWER *Geoffrey A. Dudley*	5.00
____ PRACTICAL GUIDE TO BETTER CONCENTRATION *Melvin Powers*	5.00
____ 7 DAYS TO FASTER READING *William S. Schaill*	7.00
____ SONGWRITERS' RHYMING DICTIONARY *Jane Shaw Whitfield*	10.00
____ SPELLING MADE EASY *Lester D. Basch & Dr. Milton Finkelstein*	3.00
____ STUDENT'S GUIDE TO BETTER GRADES *J. A. Rickard*	3.00
____ TEST YOURSELF—FIND YOUR HIDDEN TALENT *Jack Shafer*	3.00
____ YOUR WILL & WHAT TO DO ABOUT IT *Attorney Samuel G. Kling*	5.00

CALLIGRAPHY

____ ADVANCED CALLIGRAPHY *Katherine Jeffares*	7.00
____ CALLIGRAPHY—THE ART OF BEAUTIFUL WRITING *Katherine Jeffares*	7.00
____ CALLIGRAPHY FOR FUN & PROFIT *Anne Leptich & Jacque Evans*	7.00
____ CALLIGRAPHY MADE EASY *Tina Serafini*	7.00

CHESS & CHECKERS

____ BEGINNER'S GUIDE TO WINNING CHESS *Fred Reinfeld*	5.00
____ CHESS IN TEN EASY LESSONS *Larry Evans*	5.00
____ CHESS MADE EASY *Milton L. Hanauer*	5.00
____ CHESS PROBLEMS FOR BEGINNERS *Edited by Fred Reinfeld*	5.00
____ CHESS TACTICS FOR BEGINNERS *Edited by Fred Reinfeld*	5.00

____ HOW TO WIN AT CHECKERS *Fred Reinfeld*		5.00
____ 1001 BRILLIANT WAYS TO CHECKMATE *Fred Reinfeld*		7.00
____ 1001 WINNING CHESS SACRIFICES & COMBINATIONS *Fred Reinfeld*		7.00

COOKERY & HERBS

____ CULPEPER'S HERBAL REMEDIES *Dr. Nicholas Culpeper*	5.00
____ FAST GOURMET COOKBOOK *Poppy Cannon*	2.50
____ HEALING POWER OF HERBS *May Bethel*	5.00
____ HEALING POWER OF NATURAL FOODS *May Bethel*	7.00
____ HERBS FOR HEALTH—HOW TO GROW & USE THEM *Louise Evans Doole*	5.00
____ HOME GARDEN COOKBOOK—DELICIOUS NATURAL FOOD RECIPES *Ken Kraft*	3.00
____ MEATLESS MEAL GUIDE *Tomi Ryan & James H. Ryan, M.D.*	4.00
____ VEGETABLE GARDENING FOR BEGINNERS *Hugh Wiberg*	2.00
____ VEGETABLES FOR TODAY'S GARDENS *R. Milton Carleton*	2.00
____ VEGETARIAN COOKERY *Janet Walker*	7.00
____ VEGETARIAN COOKING MADE EASY & DELECTABLE *Veronica Vezza*	3.00
____ VEGETARIAN DELIGHTS—A HAPPY COOKBOOK FOR HEALTH *K. R. Mehta*	2.00

GAMBLING & POKER

____ HOW TO WIN AT DICE GAMES *Skip Frey*	3.00
____ HOW TO WIN AT POKER *Terence Reese & Anthony T. Watkins*	7.00
____ SCARNE ON DICE *John Scarne*	15.00
____ WINNING AT CRAPS *Dr. Lloyd T. Commins*	5.00
____ WINNING AT GIN *Chester Wander & Cy Rice*	3.00
____ WINNING AT POKER—AN EXPERT'S GUIDE *John Archer*	5.00
____ WINNING AT 21—AN EXPERT'S GUIDE *John Archer*	7.00
____ WINNING POKER SYSTEMS *Norman Zadeh*	3.00

HEALTH

____ BEE POLLEN *Lynda Lyngheim & Jack Scagnetti*	3.00
____ COPING WITH ALZHEIMER'S *Rose Oliver, Ph.D. & Francis Bock, Ph.D.*	10.00
____ DR. LINDNER'S POINT SYSTEM FOOD PROGRAM *Peter G. Lindner, M.D.*	2.00
____ HELP YOURSELF TO BETTER SIGHT *Margaret Darst Corbett*	7.00
____ HOW YOU CAN STOP SMOKING PERMANENTLY *Ernest Caldwell*	5.00
____ MIND OVER PLATTER *Peter G. Lindner, M.D.*	5.00
____ NATURE'S WAY TO NUTRITION & VIBRANT HEALTH *Robert J. Scrutton*	3.00
____ NEW CARBOHYDRATE DIET COUNTER *Patti Lopez-Pereira*	2.00
____ REFLEXOLOGY *Dr. Maybelle Segal*	5.00
____ REFLEXOLOGY FOR GOOD HEALTH *Anna Kaye & Don C. Matchan*	7.00
____ 30 DAYS TO BEAUTIFUL LEGS *Dr. Marc Selner*	3.00
____ YOU CAN LEARN TO RELAX *Dr. Samuel Gutwirth*	3.00

HOBBIES

____ BEACHCOMBING FOR BEGINNERS *Norman Hickin*	2.00
____ BLACKSTONE'S MODERN CARD TRICKS *Harry Blackstone*	7.00
____ BLACKSTONE'S SECRETS OF MAGIC *Harry Blackstone*	5.00
____ COIN COLLECTING FOR BEGINNERS *Burton Hobson & Fred Reinfeld*	7.00
____ ENTERTAINING WITH ESP *Tony 'Doc' Shiels*	2.00
____ 400 FASCINATING MAGIC TRICKS YOU CAN DO *Howard Thurston*	7.00
____ HOW I TURN JUNK INTO FUN AND PROFIT *Sari*	3.00
____ HOW TO WRITE A HIT SONG & SELL IT *Tommy Boyce*	10.00
____ MAGIC FOR ALL AGES *Walter Gibson*	4.00
____ STAMP COLLECTING FOR BEGINNERS *Burton Hobson*	3.00

HORSE PLAYER'S WINNING GUIDES

____ BETTING HORSES TO WIN *Les Conklin*	7.00
____ ELIMINATE THE LOSERS *Bob McKnight*	5.00
____ HOW TO PICK WINNING HORSES *Bob McKnight*	5.00

___ HOW TO WIN AT THE RACES *Sam (The Genius) Lewin*	5.00
___ HOW YOU CAN BEAT THE RACES *Jack Kavanagh*	5.00
___ MAKING MONEY AT THE RACES *David Barr*	5.00
___ PAYDAY AT THE RACES *Les Conklin*	5.00
___ SMART HANDICAPPING MADE EASY *William Bauman*	5.00
___ SUCCESS AT THE HARNESS RACES *Barry Meadow*	5.00

HUMOR

___ HOW TO FLATTEN YOUR TUSH *Coach Marge Reardon*	2.00
___ JOKE TELLER'S HANDBOOK *Bob Orben*	7.00
___ JOKES FOR ALL OCCASIONS *Al Schock*	5.00
___ 2,000 NEW LAUGHS FOR SPEAKERS *Bob Orben*	7.00
___ 2,400 JOKES TO BRIGHTEN YOUR SPEECHES *Robert Orben*	7.00
___ 2,500 JOKES TO START 'EM LAUGHING *Bob Orben*	7.00

HYPNOTISM

___ ADVANCED TECHNIQUES OF HYPNOSIS *Melvin Powers*	3.00
___ CHILDBIRTH WITH HYPNOSIS *William S. Kroger, M.D.*	5.00
___ HOW TO SOLVE YOUR SEX PROBLEMS WITH SELF-HYPNOSIS *Frank S. Caprio, M.D.*	5.00
___ HOW TO STOP SMOKING THRU SELF-HYPNOSIS *Leslie M. LeCron*	3.00
___ HOW YOU CAN BOWL BETTER USING SELF-HYPNOSIS *Jack Heise*	4.00
___ HOW YOU CAN PLAY BETTER GOLF USING SELF-HYPNOSIS *Jack Heise*	3.00
___ HYPNOSIS AND SELF-HYPNOSIS *Bernard Hollander, M.D.*	5.00
___ HYPNOTISM *(Originally published in 1893) Carl Sextus*	5.00
___ HYPNOTISM MADE EASY *Dr. Ralph Winn*	5.00
___ HYPNOTISM MADE PRACTICAL *Louis Orton*	5.00
___ HYPNOTISM REVEALED *Melvin Powers*	3.00
___ HYPNOTISM TODAY *Leslie LeCron and Jean Bordeaux, Ph.D.*	5.00
___ MODERN HYPNOSIS *Lesley Kuhn & Salvatore Russo, Ph.D.*	5.00
___ NEW CONCEPTS OF HYPNOSIS *Bernard C. Gindes, M.D.*	10.00
___ NEW SELF-HYPNOSIS *Paul Adams*	7.00
___ POST-HYPNOTIC INSTRUCTIONS—SUGGESTIONS FOR THERAPY *Arnold Furst*	5.00
___ PRACTICAL GUIDE TO SELF-HYPNOSIS *Melvin Powers*	5.00
___ PRACTICAL HYPNOTISM *Philip Magonet, M.D.*	3.00
___ SECRETS OF HYPNOTISM *S. J. Van Pelt, M.D.*	5.00
___ SELF-HYPNOSIS—A CONDITIONED-RESPONSE TECHNIQUE *Laurence Sparks*	7.00
___ SELF-HYPNOSIS—ITS THEORY, TECHNIQUE & APPLICATION *Melvin Powers*	3.00
___ THERAPY THROUGH HYPNOSIS *Edited by Raphael H. Rhodes*	5.00

JUDAICA

___ SERVICE OF THE HEART *Evelyn Garfiel, Ph.D.*	10.00
___ STORY OF ISRAEL IN COINS *Jean & Maurice Gould*	2.00
___ STORY OF ISRAEL IN STAMPS *Maxim & Gabriel Shamir*	1.00
___ TONGUE OF THE PROPHETS *Robert St. John*	7.00

JUST FOR WOMEN

___ COSMOPOLITAN'S GUIDE TO MARVELOUS MEN Foreword by *Helen Gurley Brown*	3.00
___ COSMOPOLITAN'S HANG-UP HANDBOOK Foreword by *Helen Gurley Brown*	4.00
___ COSMOPOLITAN'S LOVE BOOK—A GUIDE TO ECSTASY IN BED	7.00
___ COSMOPOLITAN'S NEW ETIQUETTE GUIDE Foreword by *Helen Gurley Brown*	4.00
___ I AM A COMPLEAT WOMAN *Doris Hagopian & Karen O'Connor Sweeney*	3.00
___ JUST FOR WOMEN—A GUIDE TO THE FEMALE BODY *Richard E. Sand, M.D.*	5.00
___ NEW APPROACHES TO SEX IN MARRIAGE *John E. Eichenlaub, M.D.*	3.00
___ SEXUALLY ADEQUATE FEMALE *Frank S. Caprio, M.D.*	3.00
___ SEXUALLY FULFILLED WOMAN *Dr. Rachel Copelan*	5.00

MARRIAGE, SEX & PARENTHOOD

___ ABILITY TO LOVE *Dr. Allan Fromme*	7.00
___ GUIDE TO SUCCESSFUL MARRIAGE *Drs. Albert Ellis & Robert Harper*	7.00
___ HOW TO RAISE AN EMOTIONALLY HEALTHY, HAPPY CHILD *Albert Ellis, Ph.D.*	7.00
___ PARENT SURVIVAL TRAINING *Marvin Silverman, Ed.D. & David Lustig, Ph.D.*	10.00
___ SEX WITHOUT GUILT *Albert Ellis, Ph.D.*	5.00
___ SEXUALLY ADEQUATE MALE *Frank S. Caprio, M.D.*	3.00
___ SEXUALLY FULFILLED MAN *Dr. Rachel Copelan*	5.00
___ STAYING IN LOVE *Dr. Norton F. Kristy*	7.00

MELVIN POWERS' MAIL ORDER LIBRARY

___ HOW TO GET RICH IN MAIL ORDER *Melvin Powers*	20.00
___ HOW TO SELF-PUBLISH YOUR BOOK & MAKE IT A BEST SELLER *Melvin Powers*	20.00
___ HOW TO WRITE A GOOD ADVERTISEMENT *Victor O. Schwab*	20.00
___ MAIL ORDER MADE EASY *J. Frank Brumbaugh*	20.00

METAPHYSICS & OCCULT

___ CONCENTRATION—A GUIDE TO MENTAL MASTERY *Mouni Sadhu*	7.00
___ EXTRA-TERRESTRIAL INTELLIGENCE—THE FIRST ENCOUNTER	6.00
___ FORTUNE TELLING WITH CARDS *P. Foli*	5.00
___ HOW TO INTERPRET DREAMS, OMENS & FORTUNE TELLING SIGNS *Gettings*	5.00
___ HOW TO UNDERSTAND YOUR DREAMS *Geoffrey A. Dudley*	5.00
___ IN DAYS OF GREAT PEACE *Mouni Sadhu*	3.00
___ MAGICIAN—HIS TRAINING AND WORK *W. E. Butler*	5.00
___ MEDITATION *Mouni Sadhu*	10.00
___ MODERN NUMEROLOGY *Morris C. Goodman*	5.00
___ NUMEROLOGY—ITS FACTS AND SECRETS *Ariel Yvon Taylor*	5.00
___ NUMEROLOGY MADE EASY *W. Mykian*	5.00
___ PALMISTRY MADE EASY *Fred Gettings*	5.00
___ PALMISTRY MADE PRACTICAL *Elizabeth Daniels Squire*	7.00
___ PALMISTRY SECRETS REVEALED *Henry Frith*	4.00
___ PROPHECY IN OUR TIME *Martin Ebon*	2.50
___ SUPERSTITION—ARE YOU SUPERSTITIOUS? *Eric Maple*	2.00
___ TAROT *Mouni Sadhu*	10.00
___ TAROT OF THE BOHEMIANS *Papus*	7.00
___ WAYS TO SELF-REALIZATION *Mouni Sadhu*	7.00
___ WITCHCRAFT, MAGIC & OCCULTISM—A FASCINATING HISTORY *W. B. Crow*	10.00
___ WITCHCRAFT—THE SIXTH SENSE *Justine Glass*	7.00

RECOVERY

___ KNIGHT IN RUSTY ARMOR *Robert Fisher*	5.00
___ KNIGHT IN RUSTY ARMOR *Robert Fisher (Hard cover edition)*	10.00

SELF-HELP & INSPIRATIONAL

___ CHARISMA—HOW TO GET "THAT SPECIAL MAGIC" *Marcia Grad*	7.00
___ DAILY POWER FOR JOYFUL LIVING *Dr. Donald Curtis*	7.00
___ DYNAMIC THINKING *Melvin Powers*	5.00
___ GREATEST POWER IN THE UNIVERSE *U. S. Andersen*	7.00
___ GROW RICH WHILE YOU SLEEP *Ben Sweetland*	8.00
___ GROW RICH WITH YOUR MILLION DOLLAR MIND *Brian Adams*	7.00
___ GROWTH THROUGH REASON *Albert Ellis, Ph.D.*	7.00
___ GUIDE TO PERSONAL HAPPINESS *Albert Ellis, Ph.D. & Irving Becker, Ed.D.*	7.00
___ HANDWRITING ANALYSIS MADE EASY *John Marley*	7.00
___ HANDWRITING TELLS *Nadya Olyanova*	7.00
___ HOW TO ATTRACT GOOD LUCK *A.H.Z. Carr*	7.00
___ HOW TO DEVELOP A WINNING PERSONALITY *Martin Panzer*	7.00
___ HOW TO DEVELOP AN EXCEPTIONAL MEMORY *Young & Gibson*	7.00
___ HOW TO LIVE WITH A NEUROTIC *Albert Ellis, Ph.D.*	7.00
___ HOW TO OVERCOME YOUR FEARS *M. P. Leahy, M.D.*	3.00
___ HOW TO SUCCEED *Brian Adams*	7.00

___ HUMAN PROBLEMS & HOW TO SOLVE THEM *Dr. Donald Curtis*	5.00
___ I CAN *Ben Sweetland*	8.00
___ I WILL *Ben Sweetland*	8.00
___ KNIGHT IN RUSTY ARMOR *Robert Fisher*	5.00
___ KNIGHT IN RUSTY ARMOR *Robert Fisher (Hard cover edition)*	10.00
___ LEFT-HANDED PEOPLE *Michael Barsley*	5.00
___ MAGIC IN YOUR MIND *U.S. Andersen*	10.00
___ MAGIC OF THINKING SUCCESS *Dr. David J. Schwartz*	8.00
___ MAGIC POWER OF YOUR MIND *Walter M. Germain*	7.00
___ MENTAL POWER THROUGH SLEEP SUGGESTION *Melvin Powers*	3.00
___ NEVER UNDERESTIMATE THE SELLING POWER OF A WOMAN *Dottie Walters*	7.00
___ NEW GUIDE TO RATIONAL LIVING *Albert Ellis, Ph.D. & R. Harper, Ph.D.*	7.00
___ PSYCHO-CYBERNETICS *Maxwell Maltz, M.D.*	7.00
___ PSYCHOLOGY OF HANDWRITING *Nadya Olyanova*	7.00
___ SALES CYBERNETICS *Brian Adams*	10.00
___ SCIENCE OF MIND IN DAILY LIVING *Dr. Donald Curtis*	7.00
___ SECRET OF SECRETS *U.S. Andersen*	7.00
___ SECRET POWER OF THE PYRAMIDS *U. S. Andersen*	7.00
___ SELF-THERAPY FOR THE STUTTERER *Malcolm Frazer*	3.00
___ SUCCESS-CYBERNETICS *U. S. Andersen*	7.00
___ 10 DAYS TO A GREAT NEW LIFE *William E. Edwards*	3.00
___ THINK AND GROW RICH *Napoleon Hill*	8.00
___ THREE MAGIC WORDS *U. S. Andersen*	7.00
___ TREASURY OF COMFORT *Edited by Rabbi Sidney Greenberg*	10.00
___ TREASURY OF THE ART OF LIVING *Sidney S. Greenberg*	7.00
___ WHAT YOUR HANDWRITING REVEALS *Albert E. Hughes*	4.00
___ YOUR SUBCONSCIOUS POWER *Charles M. Simmons*	7.00
___ YOUR THOUGHTS CAN CHANGE YOUR LIFE *Dr. Donald Curtis*	7.00

SPORTS

___ BILLIARDS—POCKET • CAROM • THREE CUSHION *Clive Cottingham, Jr.*	5.00
___ COMPLETE GUIDE TO FISHING *Vlad Evanoff*	2.00
___ HOW TO IMPROVE YOUR RACQUETBALL *Lubarsky, Kaufman & Scagnetti*	5.00
___ HOW TO WIN AT POCKET BILLIARDS *Edward D. Knuchell*	10.00
___ JOY OF WALKING *Jack Scagnetti*	3.00
___ LEARNING & TEACHING SOCCER SKILLS *Eric Worthington*	3.00
___ MOTORCYCLING FOR BEGINNERS *I.G. Edmonds*	3.00
___ RACQUETBALL FOR WOMEN *Toni Hudson, Jack Scagnetti & Vince Rondone*	3.00
___ RACQUETBALL MADE EASY *Steve Lubarsky, Rod Delson & Jack Scagnetti*	5.00
___ SECRET OF BOWLING STRIKES *Dawson Taylor*	5.00
___ SOCCER—THE GAME & HOW TO PLAY IT *Gary Rosenthal*	7.00
___ STARTING SOCCER *Edward F. Dolan, Jr.*	3.00

TENNIS LOVER'S LIBRARY

___ HOW TO BEAT BETTER TENNIS PLAYERS *Loring Fiske*	4.00
___ PSYCH YOURSELF TO BETTER TENNIS *Dr. Walter A. Luszki*	2.00
___ TENNIS FOR BEGINNERS *Dr. H. A. Murray*	2.00
___ TENNIS MADE EASY *Joel Brecheen*	5.00
___ WEEKEND TENNIS—HOW TO HAVE FUN & WIN AT THE SAME TIME *Bill Talbert*	3.00

WILSHIRE PET LIBRARY

___ DOG TRAINING MADE EASY & FUN *John W. Kellogg*	5.00
___ HOW TO BRING UP YOUR PET DOG *Kurt Unkelbach*	2.00
___ HOW TO RAISE & TRAIN YOUR PUPPY *Jeff Griffen*	5.00

The books listed above can be obtained from your book dealer or directly from Melvin Powers. When ordering, please remit $2.00 postage for the first book and $1.00 for each additional book.

Melvin Powers
12015 Sherman Road, No. Hollywood, California 91605

WILSHIRE HORSE LOVERS' LIBRARY

____ AMATEUR HORSE BREEDER *A. C. Leighton Hardman*	5.00
____ AMERICAN QUARTER HORSE IN PICTURES *Margaret Cabel Self*	5.00
____ APPALOOSA HORSE *Donna & Bill Richardson*	7.00
____ ARABIAN HORSE *Reginald S. Summerhays*	5.00
____ ART OF WESTERN RIDING *Suzanne Norton Jones*	7.00
____ BASIC DRESSAGE *Jean Froissard*	5.00
____ BEGINNER'S GUIDE TO HORSEBACK RIDING *Sheila Wall*	5.00
____ BEHAVIOR PROBLEMS IN HORSES—HOW TO CURE THEM *Susan McBane*	12.00
____ BITS—THEIR HISTORY, USE AND MISUSE *Louis Taylor*	7.00
____ BREAKING & TRAINING THE DRIVING HORSE *Doris Ganton*	10.00
____ BREAKING YOUR HORSE'S BAD HABITS *W. Dayton Sumner*	7.00
____ COMPLETE TRAINING OF HORSE AND RIDER *Colonel Alois Podhajsky*	10.00
____ DISORDERS OF THE HORSE & WHAT TO DO ABOUT THEM *E. Hanauer*	5.00
____ DOG TRAINING MADE EASY & FUN *John W. Kellogg*	5.00
____ DRESSAGE—A STUDY OF THE FINER POINTS IN RIDING *Henry Wynmalen*	7.00
____ DRIVE ON *Doris Ganton*	7.00
____ DRIVING HORSES *Sallie Walrond*	5.00
____ EQUITATION *Jean Froissard*	7.00
____ FIRST AID FOR HORSES *Dr. Charles H. Denning, Jr.*	5.00
____ FUN ON HORSEBACK *Margaret Cabell Self*	4.00
____ HORSE DISEASES—CAUSES, SYMPTOMS & TREATMENT *Dr. H. G. Belschner*	7.00
____ HORSE OWNER'S CONCISE GUIDE *Elsie V. Hanauer*	5.00
____ HORSE SELECTION & CARE FOR BEGINNERS *George H. Conn*	10.00
____ HORSEBACK RIDING FOR BEGINNERS *Louis Taylor*	7.00
____ HORSEBACK RIDING MADE EASY & FUN *Sue Henderson Coen*	7.00
____ HORSES—THEIR SELECTION, CARE & HANDLING *Margaret Cabell Self*	5.00
____ HUNTER IN PICTURES *Margaret Cabell Self*	2.00
____ ILLUSTRATED BOOK OF THE HORSE *S. Sidney (8½" x 11")*	10.00
____ ILLUSTRATED HORSE TRAINING *Captain M. H. Hayes*	7.00
____ ILLUSTRATED HORSEBACK RIDING FOR BEGINNERS *Jeanne Mellin*	5.00
____ KNOW ALL ABOUT HORSES *Harry Disston*	5.00
____ LAME HORSE—CAUSES, SYMPTOMS & TREATMENT *Dr. James R. Rooney*	7.00
____ LAW & YOUR HORSE *Edward H. Greene*	7.00
____ POLICE HORSES *Judith Campbell*	2.00
____ PRACTICAL GUIDE TO HORSESHOEING	5.00
____ PRACTICAL HORSE PSYCHOLOGY *Moyra Williams*	7.00
____ PROBLEM HORSES—GUIDE FOR CURING SERIOUS BEHAVIOR HABITS *Summerhays*	5.00
____ REINSMAN OF THE WEST—BRIDLES & BITS *Ed Connell*	7.00
____ RIDE WESTERN *Louis Taylor*	7.00
____ SCHOOLING YOUR YOUNG HORSE *George Wheatley*	5.00
____ STABLE MANAGEMENT FOR THE OWNER-GROOM *George Wheatley*	7.00
____ STALLION MANAGEMENT—A GUIDE FOR STUD OWNERS *A. C. Hardman*	5.00
____ TEACHING YOUR HORSE TO JUMP *W. J. Froud*	5.00
____ YOU AND YOUR PONY *Pepper Mainwaring Healey (8½" x 11")*	6.00
____ YOUR PONY BOOK *Hermann Wiederhold*	2.00

The books listed above can be obtained from your book dealer or directly from Melvin Powers. When ordering, please remit $2.00 postage for the first book and $1.00 for each additional book.

Melvin Powers
12015 Sherman Road, No. Hollywood, California 91605

NOTES

NOTES

NOTES